A Litany of Saints

Ann Ball

Our Sunday Visitor Publishing Division
Our Sunday Visitor, Inc.
Huntington, Indiana 46750

Nihil Obstat:
Rev. Frank H. Rossi
Censor Librorum

Imprimatur:
+ Joseph A. Fiorenza, D.D.
Bishop of Galveston-Houston
November 3, 1992

Our Sunday Visitor Publishing Division
Our Sunday Visitor, Inc.
200 Noll Plaza
Huntington, Indiana 46750

International Standard Book Number: 0-87973-460-4
Library of Congress Catalog Card Number: 92-61546

*Cover design by Rebecca J. Heaston; cover art after "Our Lady of
Mercy" by Jean Miraillet, Masséna Museum, Nice, France*

PRINTED AND PUBLISHED IN THE UNITED STATES OF AMERICA

This book is lovingly dedicated to . . .
Mary, Queen of All Saints;
Saint Joseph, who doesn't get the recognition he deserves;
Saint Christopher, whose story was my introduction to the lives
of the saints;
Saint Michael, in gratitude for bringing my child home safe
from war;
Saint John Bosco, my constant helper;
Blessed Miguel Pro, who reminds me of the joy of Christ
. . . and all my heavenly friends.
God is glorified in his angels and saints.

Contents

Contents

(continued))

Contents

(continued)

Preface

Saints have been venerated from the earliest Christian times. The Bible, in the Book of Revelation (the Apocalypse), mentions various kinds of saints: the virgins, the prophets and apostles, the martyrs for the word of God, the martyrs of Jesus, and all those who died in the Lord and whose good works follow them.*

During the persecutions in the Roman Empire, each community commemorated only its local martyrs. Careful records of their names and the dates of their executions were inscribed in official lists of heroes kept by the individual churches. In larger places like Rome, Christian notaries were appointed to observe and record the executions in their districts. These catalogs were kept to remind the faithful to honor and venerate their local saints. Under Roman law, up until the fourth century, the bodies of even criminals were entitled to an honorable burial, and thus the martyrs' bodies were buried with reverence by the bishops and the faithful. Thus, these burial places remained well identified. With the increasing scope and number of persecutions, only an outstanding few received an established annual feast of memorial services; all others shared one great feast in common. This "Feast of All Martyrs" was instituted in the Eastern Church in the fifth century and adopted by Rome in the seventh century. The title was later changed to Feast of All Saints.

By the third century, bishops began also listing the names of those who had suffered for the faith, even if they had lived to die a natural death. These were known as confessors because they heroically confessed their faith before the tribunals. The term has remained in use to the present day to designate male saints whose heroic virtue gave witness to Christ. Saintly women are designated in liturgical usage as "virgins," "martyrs," "religious," or "holy women."

Feasts honoring the saints, both those who lived locally and those considered patrons, were held in every Christian country with special liturgies and other celebrations. These celebrations included processions, pageants, fairs, amusements, banquets, and dancing. Countries and regions developed their own traditions to honor the saints.

Through twenty centuries of Christian history, thousands of our brothers and sisters in Christ have lived lives worthy of our admiration and imitation. The pages of a book such as this one would not be sufficient to even list the roster of those of God's saints whose names are known to us. The stories of these men and women and the customs surrounding our Catholic devotion to them provide a rich field of study and fertile soil in which we may grow an increase of our own faith.

Note
* Francis X. Weiser, *The Holyday Book* (New York, 1956), p. 77.

Introduction: Catholics and Their Saints

J. Michael Miller, C.S.B.

Most observers think that there has been a decline in venerating the Church's canonized saints since Vatican II. As our stripped-down churches devoid of statues testify, Catholics no longer seem to give the saints the role in their devotional life that was common a generation ago.

Certainly we remain attracted to the saints as models of Christian behavior. The near universal admiration for Mother Teresa of Calcutta tells us this much. Fascination with heroic lives, whether of Joan of Arc or Thomas More, has not declined. We need our spiritual heroes. Fortunately we have them in abundance. That someone can be an example to others is a commonplace in all religions and cultures. Socrates, the Buddha, and Lincoln were exemplary. But their admirers do not pray to them.

Having recognized the historical significance and example of the saints, many of us are still not inclined to venerate them, let alone ask for their intercession. Everyone can admire St. Francis, but few ask him to pray for them. Most Catholics feel no urge to enter into prayerful communication with the saints. Grudging admiration is all they can muster.

Ann Ball would like to reverse this state of affairs. In her book she gives us enough saintly "meat" to stimulate our esteem for God's success stories and to encourage our seeking their heavenly assistance. When the Church officially recognizes those whom God has made holy, she is not merely adding names to her heavenly hall of fame. She is beckoning us to honor them and to pray for their help.

Although not as vigorous as it once was, a kind of underground devotional Catholicism still exists in the United

Our Lady Queen of Heaven (of all saints, both men and angels) in a lithograph from the Cabinet of Catholic Information (c. 1904).

St. Joseph (top, with Christ Child) is commemorated with a medal designed by Norbert Schrader for the St. Louis Capuchins in 1971.

States. On the one hand, ecclesiastical documents, preaching, and mainline religious publications seldom, if ever, allude to devotional practices surrounding veneration of the saints. On the other hand, popular religious pamphlets, books, and pilgrimages to the sanctuaries of the saints tell a different story. Here the people have definitely spoken, and hagiographers are their articulate spokespersons. They bring the saints into the light of day.

Genuine popular religion plays an irreplaceable role in the life of the Church. This "people's Catholicism" is a storehouse of wisdom. Vital to such popular piety is the role that saints play as protectors of the human family. No one has more forcefully encouraged the celebration of this care through feasts, pilgrimages, and special prayers than Pope John Paul II. Devotional "props," such the chaplet of St. Anne, the scapular of St. Michael, and the prayer of St. Anthony to find lost articles, are wholesome practices insofar as they help us to love God and our neighbor more. If they don't do that, their use falls into superstition, the triumph of external form over true devotion.

Why Should We Venerate the Saints?

Should Catholics venerate mere men and women, even if they are considered to be holy and are now in heaven? Is our worship not due to God alone? True enough. We are to adore only the Triune God. At the same time, we are to venerate the angels and saints.[1] By honoring the saints we celebrate the triumphant grace of God in specific individuals who have fought the good fight, won the race, and kept the faith (see 1 Timothy 4:7).

This veneration of the saints should not scandalize us. We honor the living all the time: our parents, the Founding Fathers, sports heroes, men and women who have made outstanding contributions to our world. To honor them means to give them respect, even reverence. They have done something worthy of our admiration and approbation. How much more so have the

14

saints! They have reached the end for which we are all created. What deserves more praise and rejoicing than this?

Those who oppose venerating the saints suspect that it will distract us from worshiping Christ. But we must remember that their holiness is a sharing in Christ's grace. We meet Christ in them and through them, since He has transformed them into His new creation (2 Corinthians 5:17). Praising the saints means praising their Redeemer. To love them is to love Jesus. To honor them is to glorify Christ, who desires us to have loving confidence in His saints. Hans Urs von Balthasar comments that it is very doubtful whether "we see God any more brightly in the absence of their [the saints'] light."[2] He is right. They are God's light for us, through whom we see the Light of the world.

Do the saints want or need our veneration? Of course not. Nor are they poised to harm us if we fail to honor them. "Clearly, if we venerate their memory, it serves us, not them," wrote St. Bernard of Clairvaux. "But I tell you, when I think of them, I am consumed by a tremendous yearning to be with them." Honoring the saints with joy should inflame our love for Christ. "The memory of the saints should inspire and encourage us to achieve the enjoyment of their hoped-for company," Bernard continued. "Let us love those who love us, hasten to those who await us."[3]

To venerate the saints by celebrating their feasts, naming our children and our churches after them, and invoking their support enriches Catholic life. It is also an act of gratitude for what they do for us, a way of loving them as our heavenly neighbors.

In her wisdom, the Church teaches that it is not necessary for the individual Christian to have devotion to any particular saint, except for the Blessed Virgin Mary. Respecting the liberty of persons to choose saints for themselves is fundamental. We should never question a fellow Catholic's love for the saints just because he or she is not fond of a particular devotion, even one approved by the Church.

In matters of devotions, unlike matters of faith, a legitimate plurality should reign. Preachers and devotees of certain saints must avoid monopolistic or imperialistic claims for their saint. It is, after all, possible "to get a man without St. Anne" or to find a lost article without St. Anthony. No particular devotion is obligatory for all Catholics. You are free to pick Patrick or Catherine, Peter or Paul, John or Teresa as your model and advocate. Different intellectual and cultural milieus encourage this enriching diversity.

Why Should We Ask the Saints to Pray for Us?

It is the long-standing practice of the faithful piously to implore the heavenly aid of the saints in heaven who are closely joined with Christ. Why do we bother to ask the saints to pray to God for us rather than pray to Him directly? After all, we know the saints are not a board of appeals waiting to run messages up to the divine throne!

Intercession "means that the blessed who are one with the risen Christ are still interested in us; they can and do pray for us."[4] Unlike veneration, which is something we do for the saints, intercession is something they do for us. Just as we continue to honor others despite the separation of death, as public holidays remind us, so also can we continue to solicit the prayers of the saints. Like the risen Christ, they are alive to us. Is it not likely that the blessed in heaven are even more willing to help us after death than during their earthly life?

The happiness of the saints is not static enjoyment of a heavenly reward. Present in love to the Son, they know His mind. Since on earth they lived "for Christ" as His disciples, so now they are united with Him in bringing the plan of redemption to completion. Saints intercede for us with Christ, and through Him to the Father. They want what their Lord wants — our salvation. To seek the intercession of the saints means that they are significant for me — as I am for them. Intercession is the language of the mystical body.

When Catholics go beyond imitating and commemorating

the saints to trusting in their intercession, that is, praying to the saints, non-Catholics ring the alarm. They think that we attribute to the saints the power of answering prayers, a privilege that belongs only to God. Protestants are deathly afraid of idolatrously attributing to the saints the divine power of hearing prayers and granting favors. In the sixteenth century, the Reformers also objected to invoking the saints because the practice lacked an explicit biblical foundation. Without denying the good example of the saints, the Reformers rejected the saints' intercessory role.

Responding to these Protestant objections, the Council of Trent declared that "it is good and useful to invoke them [the saints] humbly and to have recourse to their prayers, help, and assistance in order to obtain favors from God through His Son, Jesus Christ our Lord, who alone is our Redeemer and Savior."[5] In the strict sense, of course, Catholics do not pray to the saints, as if we expect them to answer our petitions by their own power. Rather, we ask the saints to pray to God with us and for us. We ask them to join us to their prayers.

Nor is asking the saints for their assistance an excuse for our own laziness. They cannot be bribed into replacing our own efforts with their prayer. The power of their intercession for us "depends of course on the degree of intensity, explicit or otherwise, with which we participate in this act of communion."[6] Our pleas for their prayers do not get us a hot-line to God. Rather, we join our prayers with those of the whole Body of Christ that stands before God making intercession.

Among the most frequent intercessory prayers are requests to the saints or about-to-be-saints for miracles, usually physical cures. Before canonization (that is, enrolling an individual in the official list of saints) the Church "takes as a divine sign a miracle performed through the intercession of the candidate."[7] Miracles are the seal of approval upon the teaching and witness of the would-be saint. That people ask for such favors of those who have died renowned for their holiness testifies to Catholic

17

belief in the saints' intercessory influence before the throne of God.

Are the Saints Mediators Between God and Us?

Nothing is clearer than the scriptural teaching that there is "one mediator between God and humanity, the man Christ Jesus" (1 Timothy 2:5). Christ alone is Lord and Savior. This unique mediation of Jesus can never be compromised. Only Jesus Christ, through His passion, death, and resurrection, has reforged for us the link with the Father by "making peace by the blood of his cross" (Colossians 1:20).

Why then do Catholics bother with praying to the saints? Does this not involve an unnecessary extra step and contradict the Bible as well?

Official teaching is clear. The mediation of the saints "takes away nothing from Christ's all-sufficient mediatorship" but "rather shows its power."[8] The one mediator does not exclude secondary mediation, unquestionably subordinate to that of Christ. "There is nothing to prevent others in a certain way from being called mediators between God and man," wrote St. Thomas Aquinas, "insofar as they, by preparing or serving, cooperate in uniting men to God."[9] Following the Angelic Doctor, the Fathers at Vatican II taught that Christ's unique mediation "does not exclude but rather gives rise to a manifold cooperation that is but a sharing in this one source."[10]

Whether we recognize it or not, men and women are linked together. As social beings, we live in a network of interdependence. In the supernatural order, no one is a spiritual island. Our solidarity depends on our union in "the body of Christ." In this body of disciples, some are in exile — those on earth; some are being purified — those in purgatory; and some are in glory — the saints in heaven. But all of us can share in the same spiritual goods. No barriers exist between this world and the one beyond. The communion of saints cuts right through them both. Death does not separate us from our fellow Christians who are now victorious.

Every time we ask someone to pray for us we make a claim on this spiritual interdependence. Asking for another's prayers is a practice that goes back to the first generation of the Church (see Romans 15:30-31; 1 Thessalonians 5:25; Ephesians 3:14-19; Colossians 4:3). In His mercy, God allows us to help one another in our pilgrimage home. We are intermediaries or mediators of grace one for another. This reliance upon another's assistance in furthering our intimacy with God is grounded in the reality of Christ's mystical body.

If we believe in praying for one another on earth, why shouldn't we ask the saints to pray for us in the heavenly Church?[11] Christ, after all, still lives "to make intercession" for us (Hebrews 7:25). As his friends — and ours — why wouldn't they do the same? Just as they loved their neighbor on earth, so they continue to love us and to pray that we shall join them one day. That's true solidarity.

After Christ, who is united with each person through His incarnation and redemption, no one is more intimately linked to us than the saints. A "bond of confident intimacy"[12] exists between the saints in the heavenly Jerusalem and those of us in the pilgrim Church. Did not Thérèse of the Child Jesus say, "I shall spend my heaven doing good upon earth"? And we take her at her word. The saints take their whole lives with them into eternity, including their solidarity with us. That expresses itself in mediation. In the great communion of saints we still "bear one another's burdens." We ask for their prayers, and they respond.

What Ever Happened to St. Christopher?

In 1969 Pope Paul VI published a revision of the calendar of saints.[13] Since the Second Vatican Council, liturgists had wanted to prune the Church's calendar of historical inaccuracies. The experts subjected to critical scrutiny the histories of the saints mentioned in it. The Pope then included in the revised calendar only those saints who passed the exam of historical authenticity. St. Christopher failed the test. So did

Philomena, Valentine, and a score of others. Many Catholics were enraged at having their favorite intercessors dethroned by Vatican authorities. Wisely, churches, schools and religious organizations with these patrons were not required to change their names. But they did lose their official feast days in favor of saints who represented the Church's universality and whose holy lives were historically guaranteed.

Although saints called Christopher, Philomena, and Valentine probably lived, nothing more than their names could be gleaned from a careful study of the Church's tradition. No one claimed they did not exist — only that careful historical study could not affirm their existence. These "ex-saints," moreover, had never been officially canonized, since devotion to them preceded this papal process introduced in the Middle Ages. It's not yet clear whether popular piety to them will cease. St. Christopher medals are still around. And where would lovers be without Valentine's Day?

Pruning the calendar also involved changing the date of celebration of many saints. A saint's day is usually that of his or her "birthday" into heaven. If, however, that conflicted with one of the Church's great liturgical seasons, such as Advent or Lent, another suitable date was used. Thus, for example, the feast of St. Thomas Aquinas moved from March 7 (during Lent) to January 28. Other feasts had never been celebrated on the correct day. These, too, were changed. Despite the clamor, the new liturgical calendar better reflects the catholicity of the Church's saints.

"Do's" and "Don'ts" of Devotion to the Saints

In order to read books on the saints with the right spirit, we must be careful not to fall prey to certain distortions that arise from time to time in well-meaning but misinformed Catholic devotional practices regarding the saints.

The saints are not bridges over a gap that separates us from a remote Christ, as if we were unworthy to approach him directly. Most religions have supernatural figures that mediate between humanity and the inaccessible God. Saints are not influential friends in high places who manipulate a politics of grace.

Catholics do not need saints to get closer to the Lord. The Son of God himself has satisfied this need: "He who sees me, sees the Father" (John 14:9). The mediation of the saints in no way interferes with our direct union with Christ. We should not think of them as doors that have to be passed through before encountering Christ. No, through grace, we enter directly into union with Christ. To think of the saints as the middle link between ourselves and a distant Christ is to misunderstand the deepest meaning of the Incarnation — the fact that Christ became one like us in all things but sin.

In the Church's history, the cult of saints has occasionally threatened to rival the worship of Christ. In their shrines and through their relics, the people thought the saints to be powerfully "present." Sometimes the poorly catechized felt that the saints were closer to them than Christ, even in the Eucharist. This is simply erroneous.

At the Second Vatican Council, the Fathers were very aware that deviation had crept into the Church's devotional life.[14] Popular devotions, including those to some saints, sometimes obscured the primary importance of the Mass as the center of all Catholic worship. The Fathers urged "all concerned to work hard to prevent or correct any abuses, excesses, or defects which may have crept in here or there, and to restore all things to a more ample praise of Christ, and of God."[15]

The anticipated renewal, purified of all distortions, has yet to take place. Now is the time to pull from the storehouse "the new and the old" (Matthew 13:52). Ann Ball is particularly helpful in recalling for us the richness of traditional devotions to our heavenly companions. Her book is required reading for any householder interested in creating new devotions founded on Scripture, focused on Christ, and directed to the Eucharist as the source and summit of all worship.

21

Gracie Lofaro (top) is in charge of the St. Joseph altar (below) run each year by the Galveston (Tex.) Knights of Columbus on March 19.

Lamb cake (top) is traditional. Food is served and bread auctioned off for the poor, with a bowl in front (below) for extra donations.

Notes

1. The distinction is that between *latria* (Latin: *adoratio*), the absolute worship given to God alone, and *doulia* (Latin: *veneratio*), the veneration given to the angels and saints.

2. Hans Urs von Balthasar, *You Crown the Year with Your Goodness* (San Francisco, 1989), p. 212.

3. Bernard of Clairvaux, *Sermo* #2.

4. American Bishops, *Behold Your Mother*, #84.

5. Council of Trent (1563), DS 1821.

6. Karl Rahner, "Prayer to the Saints," in Karl Rahner and Johann B. Metz, *The Courage to Pray* (New York, 1981), p. 70.

7. Kenneth L. Woodward, *Making Saints* (New York, 1990), 84.

8. Vatican II, *Lumen Gentium*, #60.

9. *Summa Theologiae*, III, q 26, a 1c.

10. Vatican II, *Lumen Gentium*, #62. In *Behold Your Mother*, the American Bishops made a similar statement: "It is owing to the Redeemer that all the redeemed are enabled to share in the Savior's work, and to influence the salvation of their brothers and sisters in the body of Christ" (#66).

11. In a letter against Vigilantius (406), St. Jerome answers an objection to the practice of asking the saints to pray for us: "But if the apostles and martyrs while still in the body can pray for others, at a time when they ought still to be solicitous about themselves, how much more will they do so after their crowns, victories, and triumphs?"

12. Paolo Molinari, "Saints, Intercession of," *New Catholic Encyclopedia*, vol. 12 (New York, 1967), p. 972.

13. Paul VI, *Mysterii paschalis celebrationem* (February 14, 1969).

14. Vatican II, *Sacrosanctum Concilium*, #13.

15. Ibid., *Lumen Gentium*, #51.

Litany of the Saints

HISTORY OF THE LITANY

` In Old Testament times, the Jews had a form of public prayer in which one or more persons would pronounce an invocation and those present would answer by repeating a certain prayer. The Church in New Testament times retained this practice, calling these alternating prayers "litany," from the Greek *litaneia*, meaning a humble and fervent appeal.

In the Latin Church, a typical structure developed gradually. In later centuries, many invocations of individual saints and special petitions were added. So many additions were made that in 1601 Pope Clement VIII determined an official text of the Litany of All Saints and prohibited public use of any other litanies unless approved by Rome.

Succeeding popes approved other litanies for public use. These are the Litany of the Blessed Mother, of the Holy Name, of the Saints, of the Sacred Heart, of St. Joseph, and for the Dying. There are a number of other beautiful traditional litanies which may be used for private devotions, and many religious orders have their own special litanies.

One full form of the Litany of the Saints * consists of the usual beginning and an address to the persons of the Blessed Trinity. Next there are invocations of Our Lady, the archangels, St. John Baptist, St. Joseph, apostles and evangelists, martyrs, doctors and bishops, founders of orders, and women. There are petitions for deliverance from spiritual and temporal evils, petitions in the name of the mysteries of the life of Christ, petitions on behalf of the Church and her members. The Litany ends with the Our Father prayed silently, psalm 69, versicles and responses, and a series of ten final collects taken from various parts of the liturgy.

THE LITANY OF THE SAINTS*

Lord, have mercy on us.
  R. Christ, have mercy on us.
Lord have mercy on us.
Christ, hear us.
  Christ, graciously hear us.

God the Father in Heaven,
  Have mercy on us.
God the Son, Redeemer of the world,
  Have mercy on us.
God the Holy Spirit,
  Have mercy on us.
Holy Trinity, one God,
  Have mercy on us.

Holy Mary,
  R. Pray for us [repeat after each title].
Holy Mother of God,
Holy Virgin of virgins,
St. Michael,
St. Gabriel,
St. Raphael,
All ye holy Angels and Archangels,
All ye holy orders of blessed Spirits,
St. John the Baptist,
St. Joseph,
All ye holy Patriarchs and Prophets,
St. Peter,
St. Paul,
St. Andrew,
St. James,
St. John,
St. Thomas,
St. James,

St. Philip,

St. Bartholomew,

St. Matthew,

St. Simon,

St. Thaddeus,

St. Matthias,

St. Barnabas,

St. Luke,

St. Mark,

All ye holy Apostles and Evangelists,

All ye holy Disciples of our Lord,

All ye holy Innocents,

St. Stephen,

St. Lawrence,

St. Vincent,

Sts. Fabian and Sebastian,

Sts. John and Paul,

Sts. Cosmas and Damian,

Sts. Gervase and Protase,

All ye holy Martyrs,

St. Sylvester,

St. Gregory,

St. Ambrose,

St. Augustine,

St. Jerome,

St. Martin,

St. Nicholas,

All ye holy Bishops and Confessors,

All ye holy Doctors,

St. Anthony,

St. Benedict,

St. Dominic,

St. Francis,

All ye holy Priests and Levites,

All ye holy Monks and Hermits,

St. Mary Magdalene,

St. Agatha,
St. Lucy,
St. Agnes,
St. Cecilia,
St. Catherine,
St. Anastasia,
All ye holy Virgins and Widows,
All ye holy men and women, Saints of God,
Make intercession for us.

Be merciful,
   R. Spare us, O Lord.
Be merciful,
   Graciously hear us, O Lord.

From all evil,
   R. O Lord, deliver us [repeat after each line].

From all sins,
From Thy wrath,
From sudden and unprovided death,
From the snares of the devil,
From anger, and hatred, and ill-will,
From the spirit of fornication,
From lightening and tempest,
From the scourge of earthquake,
From plague, famine and war,
From everlasting death,
Through the mystery of Thy holy Incarnation,
Through Thy Coming,
Through Thy Nativity,
Through Thy Baptism and holy Fasting,
Through Thy Cross and Passion,
Through Thy Death and Burial,
Through Thy holy Resurrection,
Through Thine admirable Ascension,

Through the coming of the Holy Ghost, the Paraclete,

In the day of judgment,
  R. We beseech Thee, hear us [repeat after each line],
We sinners,
That Thou wouldst spare us,
That Thou wouldst pardon us,
That Thou wouldst bring us to true penance,
That Thou wouldst vouchsafe to govern and preserve Thy
holy Church,
That Thou wouldst vouchsafe to preserve our Apostolic
Prelate and all orders of the Church in holy religion,
That Thou wouldst vouchsafe to humble the enemies of
holy Church,
That Thou wouldst vouchsafe to give peace and true
concord to Christian kings and princes,
That Thou wouldst vouchsafe to grant peace and unity to
all Christian people
That Thou wouldst vouchsafe to recall to the unity of the
Church all those in error, and lead all infidels to the Gospel
light,
That Thou wouldst vouchsafe to confirm and preserve us in
Thy holy service,
That Thou wouldst lift up our minds to heavenly desires,
That Thou wouldst render eternal blessing to all our
benefactors,
That Thou wouldst deliver our souls and the souls of our
brethren, relations, and benefactors from eternal damnation,
That Thou wouldst vouchsafe to give and preserve the
fruits of the earth,
That Thou wouldst vouchsafe to grant eternal rest to all the
faithful departed,
That Thou wouldst vouchsafe graciously to hear us,

Son of God,
Lamb of God, who takest away the sins of the world,

R. Spare us, O Lord.
Lamb of God who takest away the sins of the world,
Graciously hear us, O Lord.
Lamb of God, who takest away the sins of the world,
Have mercy on us.
Christ, hear us.
Christ, graciously hear us.
Lord, have mercy on us.
Christ, have mercy on us.
Lord, have mercy on us.

Our Father . . . [*in silence*].
V. And Lead us not into temptation.
R. But deliver us from evil.

[*Psalm 69 is then recited.*]
Glory be to the Father. . . .

V. Save your servants.
R. Who hope in You, O my God.
V. Be to us, O Lord, a tower of strength.
R. From the face of the enemy.
V. Let not the enemy prevail against us.
R. Nor the son of iniquity have power to hurt us.
V. O Lord, deal not with us according to our sins.
R. Neither requite us according to our iniquities.
V. Let us pray for our Sovereign Pontiff N.
R. The Lord preserve him, and give him life, and make
him blessed upon the earth, and deliver him not up to the will of
his enemies.
V. Let us pray for our benefactors.
R. Vouchsafe, O Lord, for Your name's sake, to reward
with eternal life all those who do us good. Amen.
V. Let us pray for the faithful departed.
R. Eternal rest give to them, O Lord, and let perpetual
light shine upon them.

V. May they rest in peace.

   R. Amen.

V. For our absent brethren.

   R. Save Your servants who hope in You, O my God.

V. Send them help, O Lord, from Your holy place.

   R. And from Sion protect them.

V. O Lord, Hear my prayer.

   R. And let my cry come to You.

V. The Lord be with you.

   R. And with your spirit.

[The following prayers are said except after the Litany of the Forty Hours' Devotion.]

Let us pray.

O God, Whose property is always to have mercy and to spare, receive our petition, that we, and all Your servants who are bound by the chains of sin, may, by the compassion of Your goodness, be mercifully absolved.

Graciously hear, we beseech You, O Lord, the prayers of Your suppliants, and pardon the sins of those who confess to You that in Your bounty You may grant us both pardon and peace.

In Your clemency, O Lord, show us Your ineffable mercy, that You may both free us from all our sins, and deliver us from the punishments which we deserve for them.

O God, Who by sin are offended and by penance pacified, mercifully regard the prayers of Your suppliant people, and turn away the scourges of Your anger, which we deserve for our sins.

Almighty, everlasting God, have mercy upon Your servant N., our Sovereign Pontiff, and direct him according to Your clemency into the way of everlasting salvation, that by Your grace he may desire those things that are pleasing to You, and perform them with all his strength.

O God, from Whom are holy desires, good counsels, and

just works, give to Your servants that peace which the world cannot give, that our hearts be set to keep Your commandments, and that being removed from the fear of our enemies, we may pass our time in peace under Your protection.

Burn our desires and our hearts with the fire of the Holy Spirit, O Lord, that we may serve You with a chaste body, and with a clean heart be pleasing to You.

O God, the Creator and Redeemer of all the faithful, grant to the souls of Your servants and handmaids the remission of all their sins, that, through devout prayers, they may obtain the pardon which they always desired.

Direct, we beseech You, O Lord, our actions by Your holy inspirations, and carry them on by Your gracious assistance, that every prayer and work of ours may begin always with You, and through You be happily ended.

Almighty and everlasting God, You have dominion over the living and the dead and You are merciful to all who You foreknow will be Yours by faith and good works; we humbly beseech You that those for whom we intend to pour forth our prayers, whether this present world still detain them in the flesh, or the world to come has already received them out of their bodies, may, through the intercession of all Your Saints by the clemency of Your goodness, obtain the remission of all their sins. Through our Lord, etc.

R. Amen.

V. The Lord be with you.

R. And with your spirit.

V. May the almighty and merciful Lord graciously hear us.

R. Amen.

V. And may the souls of the faithful departed, through the mercy of God, rest in peace.

R. Amen.

Note: * From the *Raccolta* (1951), no longer a typical litany; for an updated version, see the baptismal rite for the Easter Vigil in the *Roman Missal* (1974).

All Saints' / All Souls' Day

ALL SAINTS

The Church at Antioch kept a commemoration of all holy martyrs on the first Sunday after Pentecost. St. John Chrysostom, before he became Patriarch of Constantinople, delivered annual sermons on the occasion of this festival, entitled "Praise of All the Holy Martyrs of the Entire World." The feast spread through the entire Eastern Church, and by the seventh century it was kept everywhere as a public holiday. The feast of "All Holy Martyrs" was introduced in the West by Pope Boniface IV, who was given the ancient Roman temple of the Pantheon and dedicated it as a church to the Virgin and all the martyrs. In 844, Pope Gregory IV transferred the feast to November 1. The feast was moved in order to make it easier to feed all the pilgrims; there was more abundant food after the harvest than in the spring. Meanwhile, the other saints began to be included in the memorial originally dedicated only to the martyrs, so Pope Sixtus IV established it as a holy day for the entire Latin Church.

As the prayer of the Mass states, the "merits of all the saints are venerated in common by this one celebration."

ALL SOULS

The need and duty of prayer for departed souls has been promulgated by the Church at all times. It is recommended in the Old Testament (2 Maccabees 12:38-46), and it is expressed in public and private prayers and in the offering of the Holy Sacrifice for the repose of souls. The memorial feast for all departed ones in a common celebration was begun by the

Top: St. Joseph's table at Italian festival of St. Joseph Charity Guild, Houston, Tex. Below: Home St. Joseph's altar (Bea Whitfill photo).

Saint Agnes (Santa Inés) as represented on a Mexican holy card.

Abbot St. Odilo of Cluny in the eleventh century. All monasteries of the congregation of Cluny recited the Office of the Dead after vespers on November 1, and on the next day all priests said Mass for the repose of the souls in purgatory. This observance of the Benedictines of Cluny was soon adopted by other Benedictines and by the Carthusians. Gradually the feast spread, and in the fourteenth century it was standardized for the Western Church.

CUSTOMS

A number of ancient customs associated with All Saints and All Souls have come down through the centuries, and some are still observed today. In all Catholic countries in Europe and in America, there is a general practice of decorating the graves and praying in cemeteries. In some places there are special ceremonies where the priest recites prayers for the dead and blesses the graves with holy water. In some areas, candles called "lights of the holy souls" are lighted on the graves on All Saints Eve and left burning through the night.

In rural sections of Brittany, church bells were tolled for an hour on All Saints' Day after dark. Designated men went from farm to farm during the night ringing hand bells and rousing the families to pray for the dead.

In most countries of South America, All Souls' Day is a public holiday. In Brazil, people flock by the thousands to the cemeteries, lighting candles and kneeling in prayer.

In Poland and in Polish churches in the U.S., the faithful bring their parish priests paper sheets with black borders called *Wypominki* ("Naming") on All Souls' Day. On the sheets are written the names of their beloved dead. The names are read from the pulpit during evening devotions and on Sundays in November, and prayers are offered for the repose of the souls.

Our pagan ancestors kept several "cult of the dead" rites, and some of these pre-Christian traditions became part of our

Christian feast, associated with Christian ideas. From the pre-Christian practice of putting food at the graves at times when the spirits of the dead were believed to roam their familiar earthly places came the custom of baking special breads in honor of the holy souls and bestowing them on the children and the poor. "All Souls' Bread" was made and distributed in most of the countries of Europe. In some sections of Central Europe, the boys received a cake shaped as a hare and the girls received one shaped as a hen, an interesting combination of "spirit bread" and fertility symbols.

In Western Europe, the people prepared a meal of cooked beans or peas called "soul food," which they served to the poor together with meat and other dishes. Polish farmers held a solemn meal on the evening of All Souls' Day with empty seats and plates reserved for the "souls" of departed relatives. Portions served to these plates were not touched by the family but were given to beggars or poor neighbors.

In the Alpine provinces, poor children and beggars went from house to house reciting a prayer or singing a hymn for the holy souls, and they were rewarded with small loaves of "soul bread." A special pastry made and eaten for this feast in Spain is called "Bones of the Holy."

In Hungary, the "Day of the Dead" is kept with many traditional customs common to other peoples of central Europe. In addition, the families invite orphan children to a generous meal at which they are presented with new clothes and toys. Hungarian families in the villages take turns assuming the care of graves of the "forgotten," those who have no relatives to tend them. In Brittany, the farmers pour milk over the graves as a libation for the "holy souls."

Many other customs of the ancient cults of the dead have survived as superstitions to this day. In Poland, doors and windows were left open on All Souls' Day in order to welcome the spirits of the dead who have returned for the day. In Austria, children were told to pray aloud while going through open spaces to church and cemetery so that the poor souls would see that their invisible presence was known.

Although the name is taken from a great Christian feast (All Hallows' Eve), Halloween traditions have never been connected with Christian religious celebrations. They are, instead, traced back to the ancient Druids. (See Francis Weiser, *The Holyday Book*, pp. 121-136.)

PRAYER TO ALL THE SAINTS

O happy saints who rejoice in God: After having passed through the tempestuous sea of this life, you have merited to arrive at the port of eternal repose and sovereign peace where, sheltered from tempests and peril, you are made partakers of endless glory and happiness. I beseech you, by the charity with which your souls are replenished, to regard us with a favorable eye. You are at the brilliant portals of the heavenly Jerusalem; grant us an entrance into that holy city. You are on the mountain of the Lord; draw toward you those who are yet in the valley of tears. Your feet are firmly fixed upon the rock, according to the words of holy Scripture, since you are confirmed in grace and charity; sustain those who still walk in the slippery and perilous path of this life, and who are continually exposed to the fatal falls and mortal wounds of sin. In a word, you are the saints and favorites of God; plead our cause before Him with so much force and ardor, and ask him so earnestly to associate us with you, that we may one day be so happy as to bless eternally His mercies, and testify to you our gratitude forever.

— St. Augustine

PRAYER TO ONE'S OWN PATRON SAINT

O heavenly Patron, in whose name I glory, pray ever to God for me; strengthen me in my faith; establish me in virtue; guard me in the conflict, that I may vanquish the foe malign and attain to glory everlasting. Amen.

— *Sacred Congregation of the Holy Office, 1912*

PRAYERS FOR THE FAITHFUL DEPARTED

O God, the Creator and Redeemer of all the faithful, give to the souls of Thy departed servants the remission of all their sins, that by the aid of pious prayer they may obtain that pardon which they have always desired, You who live and reign for ever and ever. Amen.

Eternal rest grant unto them, O Lord; and let perpetual light shine upon them. May they rest in peace. Amen.

Merciful Lord Jesus, grant them everlasting rest. Amen.

The Blessed Virgin Mary, Mother of God, Queen of All Saints

At the conclusion of the beautiful Litany of Our Lady, Mary is praised and invoked as Queen of All Saints because of the pre-eminence she enjoys in the Church triumphant. Her title as the Mother of God is the crowning of all the privileges, virtues, and merits of Mary.

The Queen of all Saints surpasses all others by the fullness of her grace, by the splendor of her virtue, by her heavenly glory, and by her power of intercession.

"From the moment of her conception, Mary received more graces than all the angels, saints, and men taken together !" (St. Gregory).

"Mary is the first among virgins, the mirror of confessors, the rose of martyrs, the model of apostles, the oracle of prophets, the daughter of patriarchs, the queen of angels . . ." (St. Bonaventure).

"The glory of the Mother of God exceeds the splendor of the other saints, much more than the sun outshines the other heavenly bodies" (St. Basil).

"Just as the light of the stars and of the moon disappears when the sun appears, so does Mary eclipse the splendor of the saints and angels in Heaven to such a degree that their radiance barely appears" (St. Peter Damian).

"Just as the planets receive their light from the sun, so, too, the saints receive a more glorious splendor and a greater blessedness from Mary" (St. Bernardine of Siena).

"Mary [is] raised above all the choirs of virgins in the heavenly Kingdom. In that happiest of courts, [she] has obtained the loftiness of the first place" (St. Fulbert).

"Mary's merit exceeds all others, and, so too, her reward" (St. Albert the Great).

Mary can glory in much more than all the other saints. Her

heart is immaculate, her works are holy, her sufferings are numberless; her womb bore Jesus; her breast nourished Him; her arms saved Him; her soul is pierced by seven swords. Where so many proofs of love speak, there can be no refusal.

Mary has over all saints a sovereignty of honor, of merit, of glory, of power, and of action.

Mary, the Mother of Christ, occupies a special place in the hearts of Catholics. It is she to whom many turn for the aid, consolation, and love needed when human needs are not fulfilled and when they need a heavenly mother. Just as little children sometimes stand in awe of the father of the family and need a mother's hand to hold, many Catholics are led to the Father by the hand of Mary.

In Catholic theology, God alone is adored as the almighty, the one true fountain of redemption. God is perceived as a triune God —the Father, the Son, and the Holy Spirit. For us, God is honored through his angels and his saints. Mary is a saint and, above that, occupies a special place in the salvation of mankind.

The specific type of love we accord to God and God alone is called latria. This is the adoration and love of the one divine entity. To the saints, we accord a love called dulia. We honor, love, respect them and ask their aid (intercession) because they have been set aside by God through their relationship with him. For Mary, hyperdulia is the type of love we have. Just as with all the saints, we honor her, love and respect her, and ask her intercession. Her love is "hyper," or above, that of the other saints because we believe that God, through His will, gave her a status not enjoyed by anyone else.

To consider Mary as the highest of all saints, we often refer to her as a queen. A queen is, by birth or action of the king, the most honored woman in a land. At her designation as queen, she is given the symbols of her queenship — a crown and scepter. She is presented with gifts of the best the country has to offer. She reigns over her people. Catholics consider Mary as a queen — a queen of human hearts. This does not mean that they forget the place of the King of Kings — only that they believe He has appointed a queen to assist him in His reign.

Queen of All Saints, come and establish your reign in my heart. Lead me, your humble and willing subject, to the King.

St. Joseph, Foster Father of Our Lord, Patron of the Universal Church

After the Blessed Virgin, no human was ever called to such great things, received such an important mission, or had the care of persons so dear to God, as the humble and just man Joseph. He received great graces to which he was always faithful. Living in close intimacy with the Blessed Virgin, he could not help but become more in spirit like the Mother of Pure Love. The principal source of divine love in the heart of St. Joseph, however, was his relation to Jesus. Daily, hourly, he had an almost constant intimate association with Incarnate Love.

There is a paradox about St. Joseph. Though we know he was most singularly chosen, because of his hidden life and humble occupation we think of him as being very common and ordinary. He is among the highest of saints, yet always approachable. Churches named after him are everywhere; his altars and statues abound; yet he is referred to as, and often seems to be, the forgotten saint. At Christmas, Joseph is always depicted at the Nativity, yet the songs sing of the Child and Mother, the star and the manger, wise men or kings, angels and shepherds. Joseph is there, yet hardly noticed. Multitudes carry his name as their own. His name is common even among those who do not honor him as a saint, and the English language often uses it to designate the common man — "Joe Doakes," "a good Joe," "an ordinary Joe." Again, in the army, the common "dogface" or infantryman is referred to as "G.I. Joe."[1]

Once, in speaking of my writing, my son requested, "Mama, please write about St. Joseph."

When I said that I hadn't realized he had such a great devotion to St. Joseph, Sam replied, "Mom, St. Joseph always gets a 'bum rap,' Just think of all the things he did for Jesus and

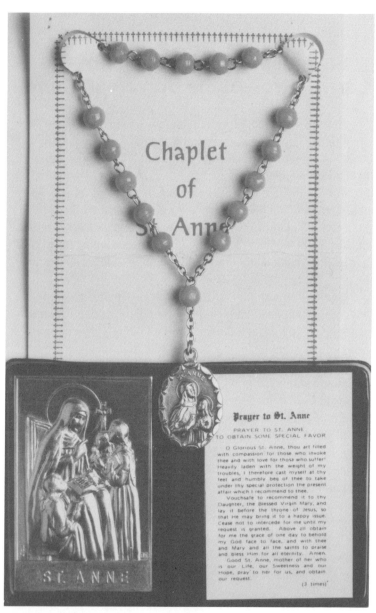

Opposite: St. Ann, painting by Georges de La Tour (1593-1652).
Above: Chaplet and pocket medal used in devotions to St. Ann.

44

Mary, and yet he hardly seems to be noticed at all. He doesn't get the recognition he deserves."

In the past century, just as the recognition of the common man's role is coming to the center of the world stage, more and more Joseph's role in the Church is being brought forward. The cultus of this saint appears to have begun in Egypt, whence it spread to the East and gradually throughout the West where, late in beginning, it has grown in intensity through the years.[2] St. Joseph's feast is observed on March 19, and in 1870 Pope Pius IX named him Patron of the Universal Church. In 1955, Pope Pius XII established a second feast in honor of this great saint, the feast of St. Joseph the Worker. Pope John XXIII inserted the name of St. Joseph in the Roman canon, also naming him co-patron of Vatican Council II.

Up to the fifteenth century, St. Joseph was not honored by a special feast of the Church and people did not generally venerate him, although many of the Fathers and ancient writers mentioned him with reverence and high regard. During the time of the Crusades, the practice of private devotion to St. Joseph spread from the Eastern Churches into Europe. This devotion was greatly encouraged by some saints of the twelfth, thirteenth, and fourteenth centuries, especially St. Bernard, St. Thomas Aquinas, St. Gertrude, and St. Bernardine of Siena.

At the end of the fourteenth century the Franciscans, the Dominicans, and the Carmelites introduced a feast in his honor into their calendars, and finally an annual feast for the whole Church was established under Pope Sixtus IV. During the fifteenth and sixteenth centuries, many religious orders and some national rulers appealed to the popes to raise the feast in rank and make it a holy day. The veneration of the saint quickly and enthusiastically spread through all Catholic nations.[3]

All that is known about the foster-father of our Lord is found in the Gospels. He was of the lineage of King David, a carpenter by trade, an "upright" man. There is no reason to suppose that he was other than a young man when he became betrothed to Mary, in spite of the fact that Western art has traditionally depicted him as much older than the Virgin.

Joseph's distress at finding Mary with child was dispelled by an angelic vision, and he took her as his wife. After the birth of Jesus at Bethlehem, Joseph was warned from Heaven in a dream to flee with Mary and Jesus to Egypt in order to escape Herod. After the death of Herod, Joseph was again supernaturally directed to return to the land of Israel. He feared Herod's successor in Judea, and thus went on to Galilee where the holy family took up residence at Nazareth. (Matthew 1:18-25; 2:13-23.) The story of Jesus as a youth of twelve being lost on the way back from the Passover at Jerusalem (Luke 2:41-48) again shows Joseph faithful in his role as guardian and helpmate. The date of Joseph's death is not known, but it clearly was before the crucifixion.

A number of apocryphal narratives are concerned with St. Joseph, but modern scholars consider most of these writings fictional. It was from these writings that the tradition of depicting Joseph as an old man stemmed.

Pope Leo XIII points out in simple words the reason for honoring and invoking St. Joseph. He was the husband of Mary and was looked upon as the father of Jesus Christ. The dignity of the Mother of God is so high that no created being can be above her. But Joseph was joined to her in marriage, and he comes nearer than anyone else to the height of that dignity. When God gave Joseph as husband to the Virgin, he gave her a companion in life, a protector and guardian, and one to share in her most high dignity.[4]

Although it is plain from Scripture that St. Joseph was not the biological father of Jesus, it is equally plain that Joseph really acted as a father to Jesus and was accepted as such by all. Most importantly, Jesus, the Son of God, accepted Joseph as His earthly father, obeyed him, and learned from him.[5]

What St. Joseph once did for Jesus and Mary, he now does for the Church, and his work is essentially a continuation of that work begun in Bethlehem.[6]

St. Joseph stands ready to provide for all who call on him. Once relatively poor on earth, he is rich in Heaven, standing ready to help all who request his intercession.

St. Teresa of Ávila was cured of a crippling disease through Joseph's intercession. She wrote, "I am full of wonder at the great graces God has bestowed on me, and the perils to body and soul from which he has freed me, at the intercession of this blessed saint. God seems to have given to other saints power to help in particular circumstances, but I know from experience that this glorious St. Joseph helps in each and every need. Our Lord would have us understand that, since on earth He was subject to this man who was called His father, whom as His guardian He had to obey, so now in Heaven He still does all that Joseph asks. Others who have turned to Joseph on my advice have had the like experience; and today there are many people who honor him and keep on finding out the truth of what I say. All I ask for the love of God is that anyone who does not believe me will put what I say to the test, and he will then learn for himself how advantageous it is to commend oneself to this glorious patriarch Joseph, and to have a special devotion for him. Prayerful persons, in particular, should love him like a father."

HIS PATRONAGE

St. Joseph is a model and patron for all. As head of the Holy Family, he is patron for families and Christian fathers. He is patron of teachers, for he himself instructed the Son of God. He is patron for the poor, for he himself lived a simple life. A patron for workers, St. Joseph earned daily bread for his family by his own manual labor. A patron of the rich who seek a better inheritance, St. Joseph had in his possession true riches and in Heaven possesses the key to God's treasury. Joseph stands as patron of travelers, exiles, the afflicted and suffering. In a special way, Joseph is patron of priests for just as St. Joseph

48

reverently carried the Word-made-flesh in his arms, the priest is privileged to bear Him in his hands.

Those who follow the example of St. Joseph in daily life, who go to him for their needs, can surely expect one last great patronage of this great saint — the last great favor of a happy death, the grace to die bravely and in peace with God and man. St. Joseph himself may have died as a relatively young man. At the crucifixion, Jesus gave Mary into the keeping of the Beloved Disciple, indicating that His own foster father had already died. We are permitted to believe that St. Joseph died with Jesus and Mary to comfort him. Thus for those whose devotion to St. Joseph emulates his humble work as an instrument of Divine Providence, his humility, his purity, his justice, his charity, then St. Joseph will be with them at the hour of their death. He will guide them back from the Egypt of their exile to their homeland in Heaven. St. Joseph who as head of the Holy Family could summon Jesus and Mary, will surely call them again to the side of his special friends at the hour of their death.[7]

HIS IMAGE IN ART

In art, St. Joseph is often depicted holding a lily to symbolize his purity, and carrying the Christ Child in his arms. The staff commonly shown is a symbol of his protection of the Holy Family. Additionally, he is often depicted with a hammer, an adze, or a plane, symbolizing the labor by which he provided for the temporal needs of his family.

CUSTOMS

Customs connected to the devotion to St. Joseph are known worldwide. When the devotion to this saint began to spread rapidly in the sixteenth and seventeenth centuries, Wednesday became a special day associated with St. Joseph. First, Wednesday was the only weekday dedicated by the Church in the votive Masses to saints other than the Blessed Virgin. Therefore, St. Joseph obviously "belonged" on Wednesday. Second, in the popular mind the ancient Station days were considered of higher distinction than the other weekdays, and since Saturday was already devoted to the Blessed Virgin and Friday to the Passion of Christ, the only day left on which to honor St. Joseph in a special way was Wednesday. For whatever reason, the custom was approved and confirmed by the Church.[8]

In central Europe, the nine days before Christmas were kept in many places as a festive season. In the Alpine sections, the custom of *Josephstragen* (Carrying St. Joseph) arose. Schoolboys carry a statue of St. Joseph every night to one of their homes. Kneeling before it, they say prayers in honor of the saint. On the first night, only the boy who carried the statue and the one to whose home it was brought perform this devotion. The following nights, as the statue is taken from house to house, the number of boys increases, since all youngsters who had it in their home previously take part in the devotion. On the evening of December 24, all nine of them, accompanied by nine schoolgirls dressed in white, take the image in procession through the town to the church where they put it up at the Christmas crib.[9]

St. Joseph is known as a patron of the married and of families. In past centuries it was a widespread custom for newlywed couples to spend the first night of matrimony, called St. Joseph's Night, in abstinence, and to perform some devotion in honor of the saint that he might bless their marriage.

In northern Spain, it was an ancient tradition for people to make a pilgrimage to a shrine of St. Joseph on March 19 and there to have a special repast after the devotions. The picnic-style meal was eaten outside the shrine in the afternoon and always featured roast lamb. The custom was known as *Merienda del Cordero* (Repast of the Lamb). For this occasion, the faithful who made the pilgrimage and then partook of the meal were dispensed from the law of Lenten fast.

On the east coast of Spain, in the Valencia region, fires are burned in honor of St. Joseph. The custom was started by the carpenters of past centuries who cleaned their workshops before March 19 and burned all the litter on the evening of their patron's feast. Today, structures called *fallas*, made of wood by boys and men during the weeks before the feast, are collected and exhibited at street crossings. These structures represent houses, figures, and scenes, many of which are symbolic of some political event of the past year. They are admired and then judged, and on the eve of St. Joseph's Day the best one receives a prize and is put aside. All the rest are burned in joyful bonfires. The celebration includes music, dancing, and fireworks (*traca*).

In some parts of Italy, ancient nature-lore rites are still performed on St. Joseph's Day. One is the "burial of winter," where a *scega vecchia* (a symbolic figure) is sawed in half. In central Europe the day is celebrated by farmers as the beginning of spring. They light candles in honor of the saint and put little shrines with his picture in their gardens and orchards. Then they have their fields blessed by a priest.[10]

In many sections of Europe, small round breads called St. Joseph's loaves (*fritelli*) are baked and eaten on March 19 to honor the heavenly "bread father." From the seventeenth century on, it was customary to have a statue of the saint on the table during the main meal and to "serve" it generous portions, which afterward were given to the poor.

ST. JOSEPH'S ALTAR

The custom of St. Joseph's altar was brought by the Sicilian immigrants to the United States. Originally, the tables or altars were family affairs, but as the Italian-American population grew, the celebrations became more public. The custom is prevalent in the U.S. today wherever there are Italian-American families.

The St. Joseph altar originated in a region of Sicily many centuries ago during a period of drought and famine. The people turned to St. Joseph, asking his help and intercession. Rains came, and their crops prospered. In thanksgiving, the community brought their prized food as an offering to their patron.

Today, the altar is generally large and has three levels to represent the Holy Trinity. The statue of St. Joseph is given the most prominent place, although representations of the Holy Family and the Blessed Virgin are often also displayed. The altar is draped simply and beautifully in white and adorned with flowers. The finest grains, fruits, vegetables, seafood, and wine are prepared, and all are invited to share in the prayers and festivity.

The St. Joseph altar is an offering of love, labor, and sacrifice. Reasons for erecting the altar vary. For many, it is to fulfill a promise or give thanks for a favor. For others, the altar is a petition. For all it is an opportunity to share with those less fortunate.

Preparations begin weeks in advance of the feast, and much hard work is involved, but all participants accept this as a form of sacrifice and a labor of love. Many hours are spent making the elaborate loaves of bread, cakes, and cookies which adorn the altar. Many of these are symbolic — shapes include the crown of thorns, hearts symbolizing the Sacred Hearts of Jesus and Mary, the cross, the chalice, a monstrance, St. Joseph's staff, fish, birds, flowers, and many more.

The meals served for the St. Joseph altar include fruits, vegetables, seafood, and, of course, pasta dishes. Often, children are dressed as members of the Holy Family, sometimes with angels or favorite saints accompanying them. The children are served first, a portion of each of the delicacies from the altar. This ritual is solemnly observed and accompanied by prayer and hymns. Guests are invited to dine after the Holy Family have completed their meal.

Originally in Sicily, the families would go out to the poor in the community and bring them into their houses. The master of the house and his family would bathe the feet of the poor, just as Christ had done to his disciples before the Last Supper. Then the visitors would be seated at the table. The poor would be served first, after which the family and invited guests would eat. At the end of the feast, the remains would be gathered and distributed to the poor. When the Sicilian immigrants reached the United States, most could speak no English and felt awkward about choosing people who did not understand the language or their custom. Consequently they selected children of the family and friends to represent the Holy Family or Christ and His Apostles. Instead of the foot-washing ceremony, the children would stand on benches or chairs while those present would kiss their hands and feet as an act of humility. Afterward, the host, his family and friends would carry baskets of food to those in need.

There is often a bowl of green fava beans on the altar, which guests take home as a "lucky bean." The custom stems from one of the famines in Sicily. At that time, fava beans were used as cattle fodder. In order to survive, the farmers cooked and ate them. Today, the bean is considered a delicacy and used in numerous recipes. It is dried, roasted, and sometimes blessed. Legend has it that you will never be broke as long as you carry a "lucky bean."

The St. Joseph's Day festivities held annually by the Knights of Columbus in Galveston, Texas, is representative of many held in the United States today. A special Mass is said at St. Mary's Basilica, after which all go in procession to the council hall for festivities and food. In 1991, Auxiliary Bishop Curtis Guillory celebrated the Mass and afterwards blessed the altar. The guests recited the rosary, a devotion actively promoted by the Knights. Then children dressed as the Holy

A typical Mexican representation of St. Ann (Santa Ana) with Mary.

Perpendicular: Shell chapel of St. Ann in the Sisters of Providence convent at the College of St. Mary of the Woods in southern Indiana.

Family were served. Guests enjoyed a wonderful meal and visited with friends and relatives. At the end, the cakes, breads and other items from the altar were auctioned, with the proceeds donated to charity.

The wood for this altar is the original wood used in the altar erected by Mrs. Gracie Lofaro. Gracie remembers her childhood in Sicily and her mother's celebrations in honor of St. Joseph to feed the poor, but she first saw the St. Joseph altar on her arrival in Texas. An older friend, who had erected one in thanksgiving for a favor, explained to Gracie that St. Joseph would help in any need if only asked. When asked if there wasn't something she needed St. Joseph's help with, Gracie replied that she would be happy to provide an altar if St. Joseph would help her obtain a house. To her surprise, in less than a month Gracie and her husband found a house they were able to afford. At first, Gracie stalled about making the altar, thinking that the expense would be too much. Also, she was busy with her young family. However, a promise is a promise, and one night Gracie dreamed of St. Joseph and an empty table. When she told her dream to the same friend who had showed her the first altar, the friend promised that all would help, and Gracie's husband began getting together the wood. She remembers all the love that went into that altar, and she is still active in the St. Joseph festivities today.

Albert DiBella told of another custom that is prevalent among the Italians and the Italian Americans. Bread from the altar is saved , and in case of danger St. Joseph is invoked. Albert said that during storms, his mother used to go to the door and toss small pieces of the bread outside while praying that St. Joseph would intercede for their deliverance from harm. It is said that those who bring St. Joseph into their life and who keep something of him with them will not suffer a violent death.

ST. JOSEPH, REALTOR?

There is an old, if bizarre, custom regarding St. Joseph that still enjoys popularity today in the United States. It involves burying a statue of St. Joseph in order to sell a piece of property. Religious goods stores all across the U.S. report high sales of inexpensive statues of the saint which people then bury in the backyard and pray for a speedy and successful sale of their property. Perhaps St. Joseph's role in selling real estate arose from his being patron saint of carpenters, but the exact origin of this custom is clouded in antiquity. Although the custom seems to border on superstition, many persons with true devotion to the saint have acted in good faith to request his aid. Blessed Brother André Bessette of Montreal is one who appealed to St. Joseph in the matter of property over and over.

For several years, Holy Cross authorities had attempted unsuccessfully to buy land on the slope of Mt. Royal that was near their Canadian college of Notre Dame. Time after time the owners refused to sell. Bl. Brother André and several other brothers and students began planting medals of St. Joseph on the property. Suddenly in 1896, the owners finally yielded and sold a beautiful tract of land to the order. Soon after this, Brother André asked his superiors to allow him to build a small oratory on the property in order to be able to receive the sick. Permission was granted, and the building was begun. The order, however, insisted on a pay-as-you-go policy, so there were often delays and halts in the construction.

A mason who lived nearby came to see Brother André to ask for his prayers to cure a serious stomach ailment; he could not eat, nor had he the strength to work. Absorbed in his project, Brother André asked him, "If St. Joseph cured you, would you come and work with me on the mountain? If you are willing, I shall count on you tomorrow morning."

The next morning the mason arrived and ate a hearty breakfast with Brother André. Brother advised him that St. Joseph had cured him and asked him to fulfill his part of the bargain. The mason obeyed, and for the first time in months he put in a full day's work.

Later, a larger and more fitting shrine to St. Joseph was begun. Because of the Great Depression, the project was stalled. In 1935, Holy Cross authorities called a meeting to decide whether to complete it or abandon it. Brother André was genuinely surprised that the authorities had doubts about the completion. He said, "Put a statue of St. Joseph in the middle of the building. If he wants a roof over his head, he'll get it." Perhaps in desperation, the authorities did as the humble brother suggested. Two months later they had enough money to resume construction.[11]

SACRAMENTALS

There are many beautiful prayers, novenas, and a litany to St. Joseph. A number of other sacramentals are connected with the devotion, including a cord, a chaplet, and a medal which today replaces the previous scapular.

In Antwerp, Belgium, in 1657, the first cord in honor of St. Joseph was made and worn by Sister Elizabeth, an Augustinian nun. She was critically ill, and her physician had given up hope for her recovery. She prayed to St. Joseph and asked for a cord to be made and blessed in his honor. After putting the cord on, she implored the saint's help, and while praying she felt her strength return. She rose from her bed instantly and completely cured. This cord was approved by the Sacred Congregation of Rites in 1858. The cord is white and at one end are seven knots in remembrance of the Seven Joys and Seven Sorrows of St. Joseph.

In 1971, a medal was struck to commemorate the centennial of the declaration of St. Joseph as patron of the Universal Church. Father Christopher Rengers, O.F.M. Cap., is the originator of the new medal. He expressed the hope that people would wear the St. Joseph medal intelligently and fruitfully to encourage devotion to the saint, to encourage unity in the family and in the Church, and to encourage loyalty to the Pope. This medal, like all approved medals, is meant to be a means of grace, an aid against temptation, and a bond of union with God and St. Joseph.

The design for the medal was carved from pine by Norbert Schrader. The plaque was sent to Germany, where the medal was struck. It is enameled with the colors purple and white to symbolize Joseph's purity, justice, and humility. A touch of red represents the Holy Spirit and the redeeming love of Christ. The medal is rectangular to preserve the memory of the scapular approved in 1893 and given to the Capuchins to promote. On the face of the medal, St. Joseph is shown in a protective stance with his arms about the child Jesus and Our Lady. The Child rests his head against the heart of the saint. The circular position of the family conveys unity. Joseph's short-sleeved garment and the chair on which Our Lady is seated remind us of the fact that Joseph was a carpenter. The petition inscribed on the face of the medal reads, "That all may be one; St. Joseph Our Protector Pray for Us." The letters GIJM stand for Joseph's fidelity to grace in his interior life and his love for Jesus and Mary. The obverse of the medal has the words, "Feed my lambs, feed my sheep. The spirit of the Lord his guide." It depicts sheep under a shepherd's staff and crossed keys, a symbol of the papacy. The whole is surmounted by a dove symbolizing the Holy Spirit. This side of the medal reminds us to invoke St. Joseph as protector of the Church on behalf of the Holy Father.

St. Joseph, most chaste spouse of the Blessed Virgin Mary and foster father of our Lord, as head of the Holy Family, call Jesus and Mary to your side. In unity with them, be my protector, my patron, and my guide on this earth until I earn my place with you in Heaven.

Notes

1. *St. Joseph Today* (St. Louis, Mo., 1974), p. 7.

2. Donald Attwater, *The Avenel Dictionary of Saints* (New York, 1981), p. 204.

3. Francis X. Weiser, *Handbook of Christian Feasts and Customs* (New York, 1958), p. 324.

4. Pope Leo XIII, Encyclical *Quamquam pluries*, 1889.

5. Ibid.

6. Ibid.

7. *St. Joseph Today*, p. 28.

8. Weiser, op. cit., p. 28.

9. Ibid., p. 57.

10. Ibid., pp. 324-325.

11. Boniface Hanley, O.F.M., "All He Could Do Was Pray," *The Anthonian*, Vol. 53, No. 3, pp. 18-28.

LITANY OF ST. JOSEPH

Lord, have mercy.
　R. Christ, have mercy.
Lord, have mercy.
Christ, hear us.
　Christ, graciously hear us.
God, the Father of Heaven, *have mercy on us.*
God the Son, Redeemer of the world, *have mercy on us.*
　God the Holy Spirit, *have mercy on us.*
　Holy Trinity, One God, *have mercy on us.*
Holy Mary, *pray for us [repeat after each invocation].*
　St. Joseph,
　Renowned offspring of David,
　Light of Patriarchs,
　Spouse of the Mother of God,
　Chaste guardian of the Virgin,
　Foster father of the Son of God,

Diligent protector of Christ,
Head of the Holy Family,
Joseph most just,
Joseph most chaste,
Joseph most prudent,
Joseph most strong,
Joseph most obedient,
Joseph most faithful,
Mirror of patience,
Lover of poverty,
Model of artisans,
Glory of home life,
Guardian of virgins,
Pillar of families,
Solace of the wretched,
Hope of the sick,
Patron of the dying,
Terror of demons,
Protector of Holy Church,

Lamb of God, You take away the sins of the world, *spare us, O Lord!*

Lamb of God, You take away the sins of the world, *graciously hear us, O Lord!*

Lamb of God, You take away the sins of the world, *have mercy on us.*

He made him the lord of his household.

And prince over all his possessions.

Let us pray.

O God, in your ineffable providence you were pleased to choose Blessed Joseph to be the spouse of your most holy Mother; grant, we beg you, that we may be worthy to have him for our intercessor in Heaven whom on earth we venerate as our Protector; You who live and reign forever and ever. *Amen.*

PRAYER TO ST. JOSEPH, PATRON OF THE CHURCH

St. Joseph! Always be our protector. May your inner spirit of peace, of silence, of good work, and of prayer for the cause of Holy Church always be an inspiration to us and bring us joy in union with your blessed spouse, our most sweet and gentle and Immaculate Mother, and in the strong yet tender love of Jesus, the glorious and immortal King of all ages and peoples. Amen.

— Pope John XXIII

PRAYER TO ST. JOSEPH, PATRON OF WORKERS

Glorious St. Joseph, pattern of all who are devoted to toil, obtain for me the grace to toil in the spirit of penance, in order thereby to atone for my many sins.

To toil conscientiously, putting devotion to duty before my own inclinations.

To labor with thankfulness and joy, deeming it an honor to employ and to develop, by my labor, the gifts I have received from Almighty God.

To work with order, peace, moderation and patience, without ever shrinking from weariness and difficulties.

To work, above all, with a pure intention and with detachment from self, having always before my eyes the hour of death and the accounting which I must then render of time ill-spent, of talents unemployed, of good undone and of my empty pride in success, which is so fatal to the work of God.

All for Jesus, all though Mary, all in imitation of thee, O Patriarch Joseph! This shall be my motto in life and in death. Amen.

— Pope St. Pius X

PRAYER FOR A HAPPY DEATH

St. Joseph, guide me on my way. Protect my soul from harm. And if this journey ends today, please come with Mary and her Son and take me to your Home to stay.

St. Anthony of Padua statue with Christ Child at St. Anthony shrine in Boston . (Courtesy The Anthonian magazine, St. Anthony's Guild.)

St. Anthony's Bread portrayed by an unknown Bavarian woodcarver (from "St. Anthony, Doctor of the Gospel," Franciscan Herald Press).

St. Ann, Mother of Our Lady, Patroness of Women and Mothers

Nothing is known with certainty about St. Ann (Anna, Anne) except that somebody must have existed who filled the role of mother to Mary, the Mother of Jesus. The real saint is Jesus' anonymous maternal grandmother. Everything else is from nonbiblical sources. But what a gigantic construction!

The names Joachim and Ann are traditionally given to the parents of Our Lady. They are not mentioned in the Bible, and historically there is virtually no information available. The names derive from an early apocryphal writing called the *Protoevangelium of James*, which professes to give an account of Mary's birth and life. This writing is probably of second-century Egyptian origin. Here the story bears a strong resemblance to the story of Hannah in 1 Samuel.

In the Middle East, the veneration of St. Ann can be traced back to about the fourth century. In the sixth century, Justinian had a church in her honor erected in Constantinople. The Crusaders brought her name and legend to Europe, and it was printed in 1298 in the Golden Legend. From that time, popular veneration of her spread into all parts of the Christian world. A feast in her honor was celebrated in Southern France as early as the fourteenth century. The feast became universal in 1584, when Pope Gregory XIII prescribed it for the entire Church.

Luther swore an oath by St. Ann that he would become a monk. But it was Luther, too, who caused the sudden collapse of her cult throughout northern Europe and then nearly everywhere else. And yet she had fulfilled so many roles over the centuries: the role of mother and grandmother linked to the increasing importance of the family from the fifteenth century onwards; the role of teacher — as in the picture by Rubens in Antwerp cathedral; the role of helper at difficult confinements; the role of witness to the dogma of the Immaculate Conception. Why is she also the patron saint of carpenters and why are so many cemetery chapels dedicated to her? The vast iconography related to her is some indication of how very important the constructed personality of this saint has been.*

PATRONAGE AND CUSTOMS

St. Ann became the patron of married women, appealed to by the childless for help in obtaining children. According to legend, she was married three times, twice after the death of Joachim, and soon young women turned to her for help in finding a husband. All over Europe, young women appealed to her:

"I beg you, holy mother Ann
Send me a good and loving man."

As gentle grandmother of our Lord, she is invoked as a helper for various needs of body and soul. Many churches have been built in her honor, and have often become famous centers of pilgrimage.

Beginning in the eighteenth century, "Ann," which means "grace," was used more and more as a favorite name for girls, and by the beginning of the nineteenth century it was the most popular girls' name in central Europe.

Other patronages of this great saint include those of cabinetmakers, carpenters, housekeepers, mothers, stablemen, and used-clothing dealers. She is appealed to by the poor in order to find lost articles, for spiritual healing, and for help in all difficulties.

RELICS

The body of the saint is said to have been miraculously discovered in the ninth century at Apte, France, when a young boy who had never uttered a word in his life suddenly spoke and said, "Here lies the body of Ann, mother of the Blessed Virgin Mary." An early legend tells that St. Paul the Apostle had removed St. Ann's body from its original grave and carried it to Rome, and that Pope Clement shortly afterward entrusted the body to the Bishop of Apte, who buried it where it was found eight hundred years later. A part of this body, a finger, is housed at Canada's Beaupré shrine.

A relic of St. Ann arrived in New York City at St. Jean's Church in 1892. That year the first Solemn Novena in Honor of St. Ann in the United States was started. Since that time, millions and millions of people have poured out their love and needs to her. The hundredth anniversary of this annual novena was celebrated in July of 1991. During the novena, the relic was exposed for veneration and was applied to the sick.

SHRINE AT BEAUPRÉ

The famous church dedicated to St. Ann at Beaupré, Quebec, is known to hundreds of thousands of Americans and Canadians. This shrine attracts vast crowds of pilgrims from both countries.

In 1650 when the little French colony of Quebec was just beginning, a group of Breton sailors built a tiny frame church in honor of St. Ann at the place where the town of Beaupré now stands. They did this because they had been caught in a vicious storm and had vowed that if St. Ann would bring them safely to land they would build her a sanctuary at the spot where their feet would first touch the earth. In 1658 the people began the construction of a new and larger church, and it was then that the first miraculous cures took place.

A local man, Louis Guimont, twisted and aching with rheumatism, came and painfully placed three stones in the fountain. He walked away in perfect health, and since that time there have been thousands of healings at this shrine.

ST. ANN'S SHELL CHAPEL

Atop a low knoll on the grounds of the motherhouse of the Sisters of Providence at St.-Mary-of-the-Woods, Indiana, there stands a small square chapel, barely fourteen feet across, dedicated to St. Ann. The interior of the chapel is walled with iridescent shells from the Wabash river.

Mother Theodore Guerin, foundress of the Sisters of Providence, was a native of Brittany and the daughter of a captain in the French navy. The seafaring people of this country have a special devotion to St. Ann, and at Ste.-Anne d'Auray on the coast of the Bay of Biscay is one of the two greatest shrines to St. Ann in the world. Miraculous favors granted to sailors by St. Ann have been recorded in the archives there since the shrine's construction in 1623.

In 1842, Mother Theodore's young congregation was living in desperate poverty. A fire destroyed their barn and its store of provisions, so Mother Theodore and a companion went to France to beg funds to support the struggling community.

On the return trip, Mother Theodore and her companion sailed on the *Nashville*. A horrible storm arose, and the ship was in immediate danger of sinking. Mother Theodore prayed fervently to St. Ann for help. In her own words, she wrote, "The wind, which blew furiously from the southwest, veered around with the quickness of lightning (that was the captain's word) and blowing with the same violence from the northwest, reversed the wave which was engulfing us and saved the ship."

The tradition of the sisters tells how Mother Theodore fulfilled a vow to St. Ann by having a Mass said in the saint's honor, by an ex-voto (votive offering) at the shrine in France, and by establishing a small chapel to the saint in the woods on their property in Indiana. A small image of St. Ann, brought by Mother Theodore from France, was enshrined here.

The first chapel, a simple log cabin, stood until the mid 1870s when it was replaced by a more permanent structure of stone. Sister Mary Joseph Le Fer, another native of Brittany, directed the novices in decorating the interior of the new chapel using designs of mussel and oyster shells set in soft plaster along the walls and altar in patterns depicting, among others, the outlines of the Nashville and a map of Indiana showing the missions established by the sisters up to 1876. On one series of shells, the story of the foundress's vow and the subsequent salvation of the ship is recorded.

This new shrine was blessed on July 25, 1876. From that date for more than a hundred years a procession on the eve of the saint's feast was a meaningful tradition for the sisters. Since 1983, a new tradition has evolved, and the celebration of the eve is now held in the Church of the Immaculate Conception.

OIL OF ST. ANN

The custom of blessing oil for the sick at the various pilgrimage places in the world is a very ancient one. Pilgrims of old used to take oil from the lamps burning at the shrine, have it blessed, and bring it home for the sick. In the United States, blessed oil is available from St. Anne's shrine in Cleveland, Ohio. This shrine is in the custody of the Blessed Sacrament Fathers and Brothers.

THE LITTLE ROSARY OF ST. ANN

The chaplet, or Little Rosary, of St. Ann originated in the last quarter of the nineteenth century. It is a pious invention of one of her devout clients. The chaplet consists of three Our Fathers and fifteen Hail Marys. The chaplet is begun by making the sign of the cross and devoutly kissing the medal of St. Ann, praying "Jesus, Mary, Ann." The first section is recited to thank Jesus for His favors, to ask His pardon for sins, and to implore His future favor. The second part is recited in praise of Mary with a request that she present the current petition with St. Ann.

The final set of prayers presents the petition to the good St. Ann. After each Hail Mary, the petitioner prays: "Jesus, Mary, Ann, grant me the favor I ask." At the end of each section, a Glory Be is recited as an act of praise to the Blessed Trinity.

Good St. Ann, help me in all my necessities. Inspire in me a greater love for your daughter, the Blessed Virgin Mary, and for your divine grandson, Jesus Christ.

Note
* Stephen Wilson, *Saints and Their Cults* (Cambridge, 1983), p. 196.

St. Agnes, Virgin and Martyr, Patroness of Girls

The name Agnes means "pure" in Greek, and this seems appropriate for the little saint who is among the foremost of the virgin martyrs of the primitive Church. Since St. Agnes is unquestionably one of the most famous of the Roman martyrs, it is disappointing that so little is known for certain about her. There is no doubt that she was martyred in Rome and was buried in the cemetery on the Via Nomentana where a church was built in her honor about the year 350 by Constantia, the daughter of the Emperor Constantine. Agnes's name and the date of her feast occurs in the calendar drawn up in 354. From then on, much was written of her, but from the contradictions in these earliest accounts it is clear that the real story was already confused. Points where there is agreement are the following: Agnes was little more than a child; she refused to marry and consecrated herself to God; when persecution broke out she offered herself for martyrdom; she resisted all threats and was executed by being stabbed in the throat, a common form of Roman execution.

In her legend, Agnes was threatened with fire and then confinement in a house of immorality. For the defense of her modesty and being disrobed before the gaze of a heathen audience, her flowing hair is said to have concealed her nakedness.

HER RELICS

The saint is entombed in a silver shrine given by Pope Paul V in the early seventeenth century. The shrine is located in the center of the crypt below the main altar of the Vatican basilica.

The Sancta Sanctorum at the Lateran is in possession of the

head of the saint. This was discovered in 1901 when Pope Leo XIII had the treasury examined after it had been closed for a number of years. Competent archeologists who have examined the skull maintain that the detention shows that it belonged to a child of about thirteen years.

CUSTOMS

Girls who want a preview of their future husband should go to bed without supper on the Eve of St. Agnes. An old legend says she will dream of the man she will marry. John Keats, in his poem "The Eve of St. Agnes," tells of a young lady who did just this — with most surprising results.

In Central Europe, the feast of St. Agnes, January 21, was considered the mating day of birds.

HER EMBLEM IN ART

Her symbol in art is the lamb.

THE PALLIUM

Agnes is from the Latin word for lamb. Annually, two lambs are blessed on St. Agnes' feast day. Since the fourth century, the lambs have been presented at High Mass in the basilica, and they are carefully cared for until the time of shearing. Wool from these lambs is woven into the pallium.

The pallium is a white woolen circular band two inches wide which is ornamented with six small crosses and which has a weighted pendant in the front and in the back. It slips over the head and hangs down in front and back in the shape of a "Y." It is worn during ceremonies by the pope, the archbishops, and the patriarchs. The pallium is a symbol of the fullness of the episcopal power enjoyed by the pope and shared in by the archbishops, and of union with the Holy See. The archbishops are buried with their pallium. The investiture of the Pope with the pallium at his coronation is the most solemn part of the ceremony, and it is a symbol older than the wearing of the papal tiara.

The pallia are made by the Oblates of St. Frances of Rome. When completed, the pallia are blessed by the pope on the feast of Sts. Peter and Paul and are stored in a casket in the Confessio of St. Peter.

Dear little St. Agnes, at a tender age you had the courage to die for your beliefs. Help me to increase my own courage in order to live a Christian life in spite of worldly pressures.

St. Anthony of Padua, Priest, Doctor, Wonder-worker, Patron of Animals

St. Anthony was born at Alfama, a district of Lisbon, Portugal, in 1195. The son of a Portuguese nobleman, Martin de Boullion, and Theresa, a descendent of the Austrian kings, he was given the name Fernando. At fifteen he joined the Canons Regular of St. Augustine, where he devoted himself to prayer and study and became a Bible scholar.

In 1220, Anthony was impressed by seeing the relics of five missionary Franciscans martyred in Morocco. He requested admission, was accepted by the Franciscans, and left for Morocco to preach the Gospel to the Moors. He fell ill, however, and was forced to return to Europe. A storm drove his ship to the shores of Italy, where he would live for the rest of his life.

Anthony attended the general chapter meeting in 1221 at Assisi, and was assigned to the hermitage of San Paolo, near Forli. There he gave the first of the great sermons which showed his calling as a preacher. He also taught theology to his fellow Franciscans. Wherever he went, the gifted preacher drew large crowds. Often no church was large enough to contain his listeners, and he preached in the open air. He traveled throughout France, Spain, and Italy. His greatest success was in Padua, where the entire city flocked to hear his sermons.

In 1226 Anthony was elected as the envoy from the Franciscans to Pope Gregory IX. Later he was released from this duty to continue preaching. He returned to Padua, where he preached until his death on June 13, 1231, at the age of thirty six.

Even in his lifetime Anthony was acclaimed as a miracle worker, and a number of miraculous stories are related about him. At Rimini, the people refused to listen to him preach

Detail from "St. Anthony [of Egypt] Tormented by Demons" by Sasetta (c. 1400-50), James Jarves Collection, Yale Art Gallery.

Top: St. Benedict, Patron of Europe, on a 1964 Vatican stamp.
Below: Twin sister Scholastica (Benedictine convent, Clyde, Mo.).

against the Cathari's heresy. Therefore, he told them he would preach to the fish. So many fish crowded the banks that the people were struck by the miracle and threw themselves at his feet, begging his pardon. At Bourges, a citizen challenged him by telling the people to watch as his mule chose either the pail of corn he was holding or the religion of the friar standing with a monstrance. As the people watched, the mule bypassed the feed and instead knelt in adoration in front of the Blessed Sacrament.

Anthony had only been dead a short while when the people of Padua asked Pope Gregory IX to enroll him among the saints. A commission of cardinals studied his life and the miracles offered as proof of his holiness. Forty-six miracles were approved for his canonization, two of which were worked during his lifetime. He was proclaimed a saint in 1232.

HIS IMAGE IN ART

In art, Anthony is depicted holding the child Jesus and a lily. This stems from a story that the child Jesus paid a visit to Anthony is his room and embraced him with His little arms. The statues rarely do him justice, however, as they make him seem soft when in reality he was a fearless defender of the faith and in his lifetime was called a "hammer of the heretics."

RELICS OF TONGUE AND VOCAL CORDS

Thirty-two years after his death his remains were brought to a basilica in his honor. The flesh was all consumed except the tongue, which was found incorrupt. St. Bonaventure was present, and when he saw the incorrupt tongue he cried out: "O blessed tongue, you have always praised the Lord and led others to praise Him. Now we can clearly see how great indeed have been your merits before God!" The tongue was removed by St. Bonaventure and is now kept in a golden reliquary in the treasury chapel of the basilica in Padua, where it is on constant display.

In 1981 the 750th anniversary of St. Anthony's death was celebrated with grand celebrations and the opening of the sarcophagus for the first time since 1350. With the permission of Pope John Paul II, the tomb was opened under the watchful gaze of a pontifical delegation, several distinguished Church officials, and about 200 others including a number of professors and doctors from the University of Padua.

Three bundles wrapped in red damask with gold trimmings were found inside the double wooden caskets. One contained the saint's habit, and the other two contained the bones and the skull. The saint's vocal cords were readily identified, as they were perfectly preserved. These are now kept in a unique container in the reliquary chapel beside the incorrupt tongue of the saint. These two great relics comprise a fitting memorial for the saint who was an outstanding preacher of Holy Scripture.[1]

ST. ANTHONY'S BREAD

The devotion now known as St. Anthony's Bread began in the thirteenth century. While the basilica was being built, a child of Padua fell into a barrel of water and drowned. In her grief the mother called on St. Anthony for help and promised to donate the child's weight in grain for the poor if the child was restored to life. While the mother was still praying, the child arose as if from a deep sleep. This miracle gave rise to the pious practice of giving alms to the poor as a petition or in return for favors received through St. Anthony's intercession. In the nineteenth century, a pious French woman named Louise Bouffier promised loaves of bread for the poor in exchange for St. Anthony's help. Her shop in Toulon became a center of devotion to the saint; the alms of those whose favors were heard were given to the poor families of the city. Today's

Franciscans use alms donated to honor St. Anthony for the poorest of the poor.[2]

OTHER PATRONAGES AND CUSTOMS

During the time of the wars against the Turks, the Christian land armies were under the special protection of St. Anthony and his help was invoked by the troops before each battle. By a special royal order of 1668, the Spanish government made St. Anthony a soldier of the second infantry regiment. At every victory in which this regiment was involved, he was given an official promotion to a higher rank. After two hundred years he had attained the rank of colonel. In 1885 he was given the rank of general and retired from active service.[3]

In Portugal, Italy, Spain, and France, St. Anthony was the patron of sailors and fisherman. His statue was often placed in a little shrine on the ship's mast, and sailors prayed to him in storms and other dangers.

Girls went to St. Anthony's shrines to pray for a husband. They lit candles and drank from the fountain in the churchyard (Anthony's Well). In Spain he was called *Santo Casamentero* or the Holy Matchmaker. Basque girls went in pilgrimage on his feast day to Durango, where they prayed in his shrine for a "good boy." Young Basque men often made the same journey and waited outside the church to ask the girls to dance after their devotions.

In Portugal, when their wishes were not granted, or when they did not find a husband, the girls took their revenge by lowering the saint's statue down a well, turning him against the wall, or breaking a bottle of wine on his back.[4]

St. Anthony is also the patron of animals. In the days before automobiles, everyone in Rome from Pope to peasant sent his horses and mules to St. Anthony's Church on June 13 to be blessed.

The words "St. Anthony, guide!" were often written on the

envelopes of mail sent by the saint's devotees in hopes of heavenly intercession with the postal service.

FINDER OF LOST ITEMS

Many explanations telling why St. Anthony is particularly known for returning lost items have been attempted, but no one knows for certain. There is a report in an ancient Portuguese book which may be historical. A man had stolen a valuable volume of chants from a monastery. Later, while praying to St. Anthony, he became repentant for the theft and inspired with a great urge to return the book. He did so, saying that the saint had made him restore the volume. We do know that the custom of praying to the saint for lost articles actually started in Portugal and spread from there to the rest of Europe, whence immigrants brought the custom with them to America.

PRAYER FOR LOST ARTICLES

St. Anthony, I come to you with anxiety about the thing which I cannot find. While my distress is as a grain of sand when considered among the troubles of others, help me to keep calm, think clearly, and search thoroughly as I look for what I have lost or misplaced. If I cannot recover the missing article, help me to understand that it is not as important as a loss of faith, a loss of love, or the loss of confidence in my ability to get better organized and to be more careful so that I can prevent more such incidents in the future.

DEVOTION OF THE NINE TUESDAYS

In 1617, a pious lady of Bologna had a vision of St. Anthony wherein he told her, "Visit my statue in the church of the Friars Minor for nine consecutive Tuesdays and your prayers will be heard." The woman obeyed and soon obtained the favor she had requested. The fame of this soon spread, and the devotion of nine Tuesdays began to be practiced by many.

Gradually the number of days devoted to St. Anthony increased to thirteen in remembrance of the date of the saint's death.

THE CHAPLET OF ST. ANTHONY

The chaplet of St. Anthony has thirty-nine beads arranged in thirteen groups of three beads each. The thirteen divisions are in honor of the thirteen miracles enumerated in the Miraculous Responsory. On the first bead of each group an Our Father is recited. On the second bead a Hail Mary is said, and on the third bead a Glory Be to the Father is said. At the end the Miraculous Responsory is recited.

THE MIRACULOUS RESPONSORY

If miracles thou fain wouldst see,
Lo, error, death, calamity,
The leprous stain, the demon flies;
From beds of pain the sick arise.
Refrain:
  The hungry seas forgo their prey,
  The prisoner's cruel chains give way,
  While palsied limbs and chattels lost
  Both young and old recovered boast.
And perils perish; plenty's hoard
Is heaped on hunger's famished board;
Let those relate who know it well,
Let Padua of her patron tell.
Refrain

To Father, Son, may glory be,
And Holy Ghost eternally.
Pray for us Blessed Anthony
That we may be made worthy of the promises of Christ.
— *St. Bonaventure*

Dearest St. Anthony, bring the Holy Christ Child to reside in my heart. You patron of lost articles, assist me that I may always be found loving my Lord and that I not be lost to wickedness and sin.

Notes

1. Joan Carroll Cruz, *Relics* (Huntington, Ind., 1984), p. 214.

2. Franciscan Mission Associates, Mt. Vernon, N.Y.

3. Weiser, *Handbook of Christian Feasts and Customs* (New York, 1958), p. 326.

4. Wilson, *Saints and Their Cults* (Cambridge, 1983), p. 272.

St. Anthony of Egypt, Abbot, Founder of Monasticism, Patron of Gravediggers

St. Anthony was born about 251 in the village of Koman, Upper Egypt, into a wealthy Christian family. After his parents died in 269, Anthony and his sister were left alone.

In church shortly after his parents' deaths, Anthony heard the words of the Gospel: "If you will be perfect, go sell all you have and give to the poor; and come, follow me and you will have treasure in Heaven."

Anthony seemed to feel these words were being directed personally to him. Providing for his sister, he gave all the rest of his property to the poor people of his village and left home to follow Christ.

Anthony lived in a deserted place not far from the village. He devoted himself to prayer and work with his hands, giving much of what he earned to the poor and keeping only what he needed for his own support.

About the year 285, Anthony moved to a mountaintop, where he lived in solitude for almost twenty years. Although continually tempted by the devil, Anthony did battle with himself, rooting out his fears, disappointments, weariness, and sin.

In 305, Anthony established the first Christian monastery at Fayum. After religious persecution abated, he established a second monastery at Pispir near the Nile River. Around 312, he returned to a cave on Mt. Kolzim with his disciple Macarius and remained there for the remainder of his life.

The fame of this holy man began to spread, and thousands of people came to ask for advice and for cures. Some adopted his lifestyle, and a number became monks. Because of this, Anthony is called the father of monasticism.

In 355, Anthony returned briefly to Alexandria to combat the Arian heresy and encourage the faithful.

At last, in 356, he died on Mt. Kolzim, at an advanced age,

105. His grave site was kept secret by those who buried him in accordance with his own request.

A good deal is known about St. Anthony because of a surviving biography written by St. Athanasius, who was personally acquainted with him. He was a man of great spiritual wisdom whose austerities of life were directed to the better service of God. His influence was very great both during his life and after his death, and veneration for him was strong all over Christendom right on into the Middle Ages.

DOMINION OVER ANIMALS

Anthony appeared to have a heavenly dominion over animals. One day he decided that he would no longer depend on his disciples to supply him with food but would plant a garden. Animals, however, began to eat the vegetables he had grown. Anthony, on spying one of the culprits, asked, "Why do you hurt me when I do you no injury? Leave, and in the name of the Lord do not come here any longer." Animals thereafter left his garden alone.

Another time, Anthony went to pay a visit to an elderly hermit in his cave. He discovered that the hermit had died and began to fret because he didn't have a tool to dig a grave. A pair of lions came and lay at the feet of the dead hermit, roaring to express their grief. Then they scratched the ground with their paws and dug out a space to hold the body. The lions then approached Anthony and licked his hands and feet. The saint realized that they were asking for a blessing, and he marveled that the animals sensed the holiness of the situation.

ST. ANTHONY'S FIRE

St. Anthony's Fire was a disease so called because St. Anthony was invoked against its ravages. It has been identified

St. Blaise as shown in a children's book (from Catechetical Guild).

St. Brigid of Ireland (after a drawing by Henry R. Van Dongan).

with erysipelas or ergotism, but it appears originally to have been a far more virulent and contagious disorder. The disease is produced by eating a poisonous fungus which grows on rye. It takes the form of an inflammation of the skin accompanied by fever, burning sensations, convulsions, and gangrene. Anthony is still invoked against diseases of the skin.

All or part of St. Anthony's relics were translated in the eleventh century to Mota in the French district of the Viennois, and the event coincided with local outbreaks of ergotism. The saint's shrine gained the reputation of affording a remedy for this disease, although later its efficacy was extended to other diseases. At the shrine, wine was poured over the relics and administered to the patients in small amounts. An order of hospitalers, afterwards canons regular, of St. Anthony was founded to look after sufferers of the disease. This order is now extinct.[1] The Order of Hospitalers of St. Anthony administered his shrine in the Viennois and raised income from it. This was augmented by begging expeditions, when much was made of the saint's "punishing" powers.[2]

(During the Middle Ages, monasteries were vulnerable, especially in times of disorder and war. Often the identification of the monastery with its protective saint could be a crucial means of defense. Saints were thought of as protectors, and the monks cultivated the general idea that saints were to be feared as well as loved.

("We worship saints for fear," wrote William Tyndale, "lest they should be displeased and angry with us and plague us or hurt us. . . . Who dare deny St. Anthony a fleece of wool for fear of his terrible fire, or lest he send the pox among our sheep?"[3])

EMBLEMS IN ART

In art, St. Anthony's symbols are the bell and a pig.

PRAYER FOR A MIRACLE

Most holy St. Anthony, gentlest of saints, your love of God and charity for his creatures made you worthy, while on earth, to possess miraculous powers. Encouraged by this I implore you to obtain for me this request. You are the Saint of Miracles, Blessed Anthony, and your heart was ever full of sympathy. Present my petition to Jesus, and the gratitude of my heart will be ever yours.

A PRAYER

O glorious St. Anthony, who, upon hearing only one word of the holy Gospel whilst assisting at the divine Liturgy, didst forsake the riches and ease of thy father's house, thy native land, and the world, in order to retire into the wilderness; who, notwithstanding the heavy burden of years and the ravages of a lifetime of penance, didst not hesitate to leave thy solitude and go up to Alexandria in Egypt to reproach openly the impiety of heretics and to strengthen the wavering faith of Christians, as a true confessor of Jesus Christ, eager to receive the palm of martyrdom, had thy Lord permitted it; ah, get us the grace to be ever zealous in the cause of Jesus Christ and of His Church, and to persevere even to the end of our days in our adherence to Catholic truth, in the observance of His commandments, in the practice of His counsels and in the imitation of thy virtues; that so, having faithfully followed thine example here on earth, we may come to marvel at thy glory in Heaven and to be partakers of the same, through all the ages. Amen. Our Father, Hail Mary, Glory Be, three times.
— *The Raccolta*

St. Anthony, although you were faithful to the demands that those in the world who needed you laid on your time, you found your greatest joy in solitude, alone with your God. Help me remember, in the hustle and bustle of everyday life, to take a few moments daily for my own solitude in company with God.

Notes

1. Wilson, *Saints and Their Cults* (Cambridge, 1983), p. 19.
2. Ibid., p. 29.
3. Ibid., p. 31.

St. Benedict, Patriarch of Western Monks and Patron of Europe

St. Benedict, founder of the Benedictine Order, was born at Nursia, Italy about 480, and died at Monte Cassino in 548. Few particulars are known of the life of this man whose monastic rule and the monks who followed it have been so influential in western culture.

Benedict was sent to Rome as a student, but the corrupt life he saw there drove him, at twenty, to become a solitary at Subiaco. Later, a community of monks requested he come to be their abbot, which he did, but his standards were so high that it was not a peaceful arrangement. There was apparently even an attempt on his life by placing poison in his wine. But when he made the sign of the cross over his cup, as was his custom, it broke into pieces.

Returning to Subiaco, he organized twelve small communities in various places, and around 529 he established the monastery of Monte Cassino, becoming its abbot. Here he drew up his monastic rule, basing it partially on that of St. Basil. His fame as a wonder-worker spread rapidly, even during his lifetime.

When he knew he was dying, Benedict was carried into the chapel to receive Communion and died standing erect, supported by his fellow monks. He was buried in the same grave as his sister, St. Scholastica.

From examining his Holy Rule, we can infer the type of man Benedict was: a man of peace and moderation, a loving father who insisted on good discipline with respect for human personality and individual capabilities, a practical and composed man. Benedict called his rule a "school of the Lord's service, in which we hope to order nothing harsh or rigorous."

This saint had a profound veneration for the Holy Cross and performed many miracles by its means. He taught his followers to have great reverence for the cross, the sign of our redemption, and to rely on its use in combating the world, the flesh, and the devil.

To a large extent, European culture spread from the medieval monasteries of the Benedictines. Under his rule, the tradition of monastic teaching in the West was pioneered by the monks. St. Benedict has even been called the Father of Europe and was named its first patron in 1964 by Pope Paul VI.

THE RULE OF ST. BENEDICT

Benedict's rule is a masterpiece of simplicity and moral guidance, written "that in all things God may be glorified." He begins with the love of God and of neighbor, as Christ had commanded. He incorporates the Ten Commandments and continues with intensely practical advice for his monks. His final admonition reminds the reader: "never to despair of God's mercy."

Benedict worked to eliminate the deeply rooted prejudice against manual work that in his time was considered degrading, the province of slaves. He believed that labor was not only dignified but a great disciplinary force for human nature. Work was compulsory for those who joined his community, whose motto has always been *Ora et Labora* (Pray and Work).

HIS EMBLEMS IN ART

In art, Benedict is portrayed with a broken cup and a raven. A legend tells that Benedict befriended a raven that used to come out of the woods to receive meals from him. Once, when an envious priest tried to kill Benedict with a poisonous loaf of bread, the faithful raven carried it off and hid it. The cup is symbolic of the cup of poisoned wine that broke after his blessing.

PATRONAGES

Benedict is invoked for the healing of fevers, inflammatory diseases, and kidney problems. He is also called on by those seeking faith. His protection is asked against poison.

THE MEDAL OF ST. BENEDICT

Much of the origin and early history of this medal is hidden in the twilight of antiquity. The medal of St. Benedict is one of the oldest sacramentals used in the Church. Because of the extraordinary number of miraculous occurrences, both physical and spiritual, attributed to this medal, it became popularly known as the "devil-chasing medal."

On the face of the medal is an image of St. Benedict standing before an altar. He holds the cross in one hand and the Benedictine Rule in the other. On either side of the altar are an eagle and the traditional chalice. Inscribed in small letters beside two columns are the words *Crux S. Patris Benedicti* (Cross of Holy Father Benedict). Written in larger letters in a circular margin of the medal are the words *Ejus in obitu nostro praesentia muniamur* (May we be protected in our death by his presence). St. Benedict is considered one of the patrons of the dying because of the circumstances of his own happy death. Below the figure of the saint on today's medals is the year the medal was struck — 1880. This is known as the Jubilee medal as it was struck to commemorate the fourteenth centenary of the birth of the saint. Near this is the Monte Cassino inscription, the abbey where the medal was struck.

The back of the medal has a cross of St. Benedict surmounted by the word *Pax* (Peace), the Benedictine motto, and a circular margin which bears the inscription VRSNSMVSMQLIVB. This stands for: *Vade Retro Satana* (Get thee behind me Satan), *Nunquam Suade Mihi Vana* (Persuade me not to vanity), *Sunt Mala Quae Libas* (The cup you offer is evil), and *Ipse Venena Bibas* (Drink the poison yourself). On the upright bar of the cross are found the letters C.S.S.M.L., which stand for *Crux Sacra Sit Mihi Lux* (May the Holy Cross be my light) and on the horizontal bar of the cross N.D.S.M.D., *Non Draco Sit Mihi Dux* (Let not the devil be my guide). The four large letters around the arms of the cross stand for *Crux Sancti Patris Benedicti* (Cross of Holy Father Benedict). The older version of the medal-cross carried the letters U.I.O.G.D., which stand for *Ut In Omnes Gloriam Deum* (That in all things God be glorified).

Shortly after the year 1000, a saintly youth named Bruno was miraculously cured of a deadly snakebite by the Cross of St. Benedict. In 1048, this young Benedictine became Pope Leo IX. His reign marked the end of a deplorable period in the history of the papacy. As Pope, St. Leo IX carried out vigorous reforms of the clergy and prepared the way for future popes to be elected by the cardinals of the Roman Church alone. He did much to spread the devotion to the Holy Cross and to St. Benedict. He enriched the medal of St. Benedict, which replaced the Cross of St. Benedict, with many blessings and indulgences. A later Pope, Benedict XIV, gave the solemn approval of the Church to the use of this medal and urgently recommended it to all the faithful.

The life of St. Benedict was characterized by a powerful, all-embracing love for God, a serene dedication to a life based on prayer, and absolute trust in the providence of God. The medal of this saint acts as a reminder to the wearer of those virtues that the saint practiced during his life; it serves as a substantial outward sign of the person's interior commitment to a life marked by a constant prayerful disposition, trust in God, and charity.

The wearing of the medal is in itself an unspoken prayer, a plea for heavenly protection and a loving token of our attachment to God.

The medal of St. Benedict may be worn or carried. No special prayers are prescribed, but the wearer should cherish a special devotion to Christ Crucified and have great confidence in St. Benedict.

PRAYER FOR SEEKERS OF FAITH

Gracious and holy Father, give us the wisdom to discover You, the intelligence to understand You, the diligence to seek after You, the patience to wait for You, eyes to behold You, a heart to meditate on You, and a life to proclaim You, through the power of the spirit of Jesus, our Lord.
— *St. Benedict*

ST. SCHOLASTICA, HIS TWIN SISTER

As with Benedict, practically nothing is known of St. Scholastica's early life other than that she was his twin sister. Their parents were Christian patricians, nobles who apparently put no obstacles in the way of their children when they desired to give themselves completely to God. The love of order, seclusion, prayer, charity, and hospitality which characterizes the lives of these twin saints was apparently fostered in a Christian home.

In all probability, she was not baptized with the name Scholastica for there was then no saint of that name and the name means "scholar" or "disciple." The name was probably given to her because she was her brother's scholar in his "School of the Lord's Service," as he termed the monastic life.

Scholastica was apparently dedicated to God at an early age, although she probably continued living at home. There is a tradition that she founded, in collaboration with her brother, and governed a community of nuns at Plombariola, about five miles from his own monastery, although no historical documents or ruins remain to confirm its location. Some scholars believe her convent was a kind of hermitage with only

Opposite: St. Christopher, carved in marble by F. A. Klein, Jr. Above: Christopher medal awarded for outstanding films, books, TV shows.

a few religious near the base of Monte Cassino where an ancient church dedicated to her now stands.

St. Scholastica apparently had a joyous nature and lived simply in an intense mystical union with God. The last antiphon for the vespers of her feast announced: "She could do more because she loved more!"

According to the writings of St. Gregory, it was customary for St. Benedict and St. Scholastica to meet once a year at a house about halfway between the monastery and the convent to spend a day together in prayer and spiritual conversation. This was an occasion of mutual encouragement and support. On one such occasion, which proved to be the last, the saintly pair had spent the day as usual and together with their companions had just finished their evening meal. The time for parting was at hand, and Scholastica, perhaps sensing her impending death, asked her brother to continue the discussion and postpone his return to the monastery until the next morning.

Benedict, disciplined monk that he was, refused. Thereupon, Scholastica had recourse to a higher power. She bent her head and prayed that God would answer her petition. As soon as she raised her head, a torrential storm began, making it impossible for Benedict and his monks to leave.

In astonishment, Benedict looked at his sister and exclaimed, "What have you done?"

Laughingly, Scholastica replied, "I asked a favor of you and you refused. I asked my Lord and He has granted my petition! Go now, brother! Go, if you can!"

Needless to say, Benedict had no alternative but to yield to his sister's wishes, and they resumed their discourse, spending the entire night in delightful conversation on spiritual things.

Three days later, the significance of this miracle was understood more clearly when he was favored with a vision in which he saw the soul of his sister winging its flight to Heaven in the form of a dove. He announced her death to his community, thanking God for the eternal happiness of his sister.

Benedict arranged for Scholastica's burial in the tomb he

had prepared for himself, and where he himself was laid only a few weeks later. Thus, in death as in life, the brother and sister remained closely united.

In art, Scholastica is represented as a Benedictine Abbess, with the dove as her emblem. She is also shown with a crosier in recognition of her authority over her first spiritual daughters, and she is counted as the foundress of the Benedictine nuns. Sometimes she is shown with a book representing the Holy Rule, or with a lily and a crucifix. Occasionally she is pictured with a small child at her feet because she is invoked for the little ones against convulsions and colic. She is also invoked by expectant mothers for a happy delivery. Most artists have represented St. Scholastica as youthful in appearance, although in so doing they idealize her, for she died at an advanced age. Perhaps because of the miracle associated with her, Scholastica is often invoked against storms.

Holy Benedict and Scholastica, in addition to your love of God you shared a strong filial devotion which worked in a complimentary manner for the good of each of you. Help me to promote love and mutual aid between my own brothers and sisters, both those in my family and in my extended family, all brothers and sisters in Christ.

St. Blaise, Physician, Bishop, Martyr, Patron of Those With Throat Diseases

There is said to have been a bishop of Sebaste in Armenia named Blaise who was martyred, perhaps under Licinius at the beginning of the fourth century. The traditional account of him is late and mentions many marvels and tortures, with all the historical particulars lacking. His cultus spread rapidly from the eighth century onward in both the East and the West. He was invoked especially on behalf of diseased creatures, human and animal alike, because of some of the miracles attributed to him.

In art, Blaise is shown dressed as a bishop with a crozier. He sometimes is depicted with the instruments of his passion, a comb, hooks, or two crossed candles. His name is spelled variously as Blaise, Blase, Blazey, Blasius, and sometimes otherwise.

According to his legend, Blaise was from a wealthy family. He spent his early years studying philosophy and later became a physician. He was ordained and made Bishop of Sebaste. During the persecution of Licinius, he retreated to a cave on Mt. Argeus and became a hermit. Here he befriended wild animals and cared for them when they were wounded or sick. Hunters found him in the woods, and he was seized and carried off to prison by order of the governor of Cappadocia and Lower Armenia, Agricolus. At the prison, a mother implored his help for her child, who was choking on a fish bone. The child was cured, and since that time Blaise's aid has been solicited for any throat ailments. Agricolus failed in several attempts to make Blaise apostatize. He was cruelly tortured by tearing his flesh with hooks and iron combs. He was finally beheaded about the year 316. The candles used in the blessing of throats are commemorative of the tapers Blaise was given to dispel the gloom of his prison cell.

Blaise became one of the most popular saints of the Middle

Ages. Legends relate how, shortly before his death, he asked God for the power of curing all those who would pray to him for help. In medieval times, there were many shrines erected in his honor. The Abbey of St. Blasius in the Black Forest and numerous other places claim to have some of his relics.

In central Europe and the Latin countries, the people are given blessed breads called *Pan bendito* or St. Blaise sticks. They eat a small piece of this bread whenever they have a sore throat.

THE BLESSING OF THROATS

The blessing of the throats is a custom that is centuries old, a ritual adopted by the Church as one of its official blessings. On the saint's feast day, February 3, the priest holds two crossed candles against the head or throat of the person and says, "Through the intercession of St. Blaise, bishop and martyr, may the Lord free you from evils of the throat and from any other evil." In some parts of Italy, instead of using the blessed candles, the priest touches the throat of the faithful with a wick dipped in blessed oil while he pronounces the invocation.

PRAYER TO ST. BLAISE

O glorious St. Blaise, who by thy martyrdom didst leave to the Church a precious witness to the faith, obtain for us the grace to preserve within ourselves this divine gift, and to defend, without human respect, both by word and example, the truth of that same faith which is so wickedly attacked and slandered in these our times. Thou who didst miraculously restore a little child at the point of death by reason of an affliction of the throat, grant us thy mighty protection in like misfortunes; and, above all, obtain for us the grace of Christian mortification together with a faithful observance of the precepts of the Church, which may keep us from offending Almighty God. Amen.

St. Blaise, free me from any affliction of the throat, and save me from all evil.

St. Brigid, Foundress, Wonder-worker, Patroness of Ireland

Brigid grew up in the fifth century when the great St. Patrick was Christianizing Ireland. She became associated with one of Patrick's followers and fellow bishops, and under his authority she became a nun and founded a famous convent at Kildare. The community grew rapidly, and soon her sisters were spread throughout the land. Brigid is looked upon as the initiator and abbess of the first women's religious community in Ireland.

On the Emerald Isle, devotion to St. Brigid, the "Mary of the Gael," is second only to that of the great St. Patrick himself. Ascertainable facts about her life, however, are few. Numerous accounts were written during the centuries immediately after her death, but these consist principally of miracles and anecdotes which are mixed liberally with folklore. They do give the impression, however, of a strong, merry, compassionate person imbued with a shining charity. She seems to have had a unique position in the Irish Church even during her lifetime. Brigid's cultus spread far beyond her native land. In England and Scotland, churches were dedicated in her honor as St. Bride. In Wales she is known as Ffraid Santes.

Most of the wonders related of Brigid emphasize her charity; her miracles met the spiritual and physical needs of her neighbors. One miracle story the Irish love to tell about Brigid, who was called the "wonder-worker," is that while she was sitting with a blind nun one afternoon, the sunset was so beautiful that Brigid was moved with pity that her companion could not see. She touched the blind nun's eyes and sight was restored. Surprisingly, the nun was not pleased and asked Brigid to make her blind again, telling her that "when the world is so visible to the eyes, God is less clear to the soul."

CUSTOMS

In the highlands of Scotland, St. Brigid's feast (February 1) is St. Bride's Day. In the Hebrides, the servants took a sheaf of oats, dressed it up in women's clothes, put it in a basket, and laid a club by it to see if there was an imprint of the club the next morning. If so, St. Brigid had come by in the night and there would be a good harvest. In other parts, families made a bed of corn and hay over which some blankets were thrown. They then went out and called three times "Brigid, Brigid, come in, thy bed is ready." They left candles burning near it all night. These customs may stem from old superstitions connected with Brigit the Celtic goddess of fire and crops.[1]

A woman's special privilege of proposing in leap years is traced to an old story about St. Brigid and St. Patrick. In their day, celibacy was not mandatory for either priests or nuns. The story says Brigid came to Patrick in tears saying that there was much unrest and anxiety among her women because of the unfair custom that prohibited women from taking the initiative in matrimony. Patrick, sternly celibate himself, sympathetically offered to grant the ladies the right to do their own proposing one full year of each seven. Evidently a good bargainer, Brigid talked him into one year out of each four, and the longest one at that!

As soon as the agreement was in effect, Brigid proposed to Patrick. He begged off on grounds he had taken a vow of celibacy, but his natural gallantry made him soften his refusal by giving Brigid a kiss and a silk gown. Up until the last century, it was an unwritten law in the British Isles that any man had to pay a forfeiture of a silk dress to the lady he turned down during leap year.[2]

St. Brigid, teach me to imitate your joy in charity to my neighbor.

Notes

1. Sir James Frazer, *The Golden Bough* (New York, 1940), p.74-75.

2. Howard Harper, *Days and Customs of All Faiths* (New York, 1957), p. 60.

Fresco in the convent of St. Clare, Assisi, where the body of the saint, declared universal patron of television by Pope Paul VI, is interred.

St. Dymphna, as she is portrayed at the U. S. National Shrine of St. Dymphna, at the Massillon Psychiatric Center, Massillon, Ohio.

St. Christopher, Martyr, Patron of Travelers

Practically nothing is known about this popular saint other than his name and the fact of his martyrdom, probably about the third century. Although his veneration was widespread in both the Eastern and Western Church from the earliest centuries, it was early legends that supplied with abundant fantasy what history could not provide; all manner of startling details were told of him.

A LEGENDARY SAINT

A pious and most popular legendary biography of Christopher is found in the thirteenth-century *Golden Legend*. This legend tells of a heathen king who, through the prayers of his wife to the Blessed Virgin, had a son whom he named Offerus. This young man grew to great size and strength. The boy decided to serve only the strongest lord in the world, so he began in the service of an emperor. Discovering the emperor was frightened of the Devil, Offerus then served the Devil for a while, until he saw how the Devil trembled at the sight of a crucifix. Thus the young giant determined to serve Christ and, asking advice from a hermit, was instructed to make a home by a deep and treacherous river and carry Christian pilgrims across.

One night a little boy asked to be carried, so Offerus placed the child on his shoulders and entered the churning water. As he forded the river, the child became heavier and heavier until Offerus thought he would fail. When he reached the other side, he asked with surprise why the child was so heavy. The child replied that he had carried not only the whole world but Him who had made it. The child identified Himself as Christ, then took Offerus into the water and baptized him, giving him the name of Christopher, or Christ-bearer. He instructed the saint to place his staff into the ground, and it immediately burst forth into leaves and blossoms as the Christ child disappeared. Christopher later went joyfully to persecution and death for his beloved Lord. One account of his martyrdom has him being shot with arrows for twelve hours and finally beheaded.

DEVOTIONS AND PATRONAGES

The legends inspired many devotions. St. Christopher was venerated as a patron against sudden and unexpected death, especially during the times of epidemics and plagues. The faithful believed that by praying before his ikon in the morning, no harm would come to them that day. The custom began of hanging his picture over the door of the house or painting it on the walls outside so that others could also venerate the saint. Christopher is the patron of ferryboats, pilgrims, travelers, and freight ships. He is counted among the patrons of gardeners from his legendary staff bursting into bloom. He is also known as a patron of skiing. One of the most famous ski resorts in Austria, Sankt Christoph am Arlberg, is named for the saint.

Churches and monasteries were dedicated to St. Christopher as early as 532. A breviary from the early seventh century has a special office in his honor. In 1386, a brotherhood was founded under his patronage in Tyrol and Vorarlberg to guide travelers over the Arlberg. Temperance societies were established in his name as early as 1517.

Although coins with his image are from a much earlier period, use of the medals and plaques which people now carry on key chains or in their cars began in the sixteenth century. Their original purpose was to serve as a picture of the saint for travelers to gaze on in the morning and to protect them from sudden death that day. Although the original custom has long died out, the medals remain as a token of St. Christopher's help and protection in modern traffic. In the early part of this century, Christopher's patronage of automobiles became so popular that non-Catholics as well as Catholics kept the medals in their cars. In many countries, it was a custom to bless automobiles on his feast day.

In 1969 Christopher's feast was dropped from the Universal Calendar, and the Church no longer promotes his cult. His name lives on in this country, however, in a society founded by Father James Keller, M.M., to promote Christian principles (see Father John Catoir, *The Christophers*, in the appendix "Correspondence and Thank You").

Blessed St. Christopher, patron of travelers, assist me in my travels through life. Guide me through the byways of love, peace, and justice to join the main road to Heaven.

St. Clare, Foundress, Patroness of Television

St. Clare is the foundress of the Franciscan order of women known as Poor Clare Nuns. Part of her fame is reflected from her famous friend and townsman, St. Francis of Assisi, whose co-worker she was.

These two young Italians were much alike, bringing happiness to their religion in an age when Christians tended to be somber.

Clare came from a wealthy family. When she was only seventeen or eighteen, she ran away from home to become a follower of St. Francis. He received her profession as a nun, and on Palm Sunday 1212 they founded the Order of Poor Ladies, later called Poor Clares. Clare's two sisters and her widowed mother joined her in the order. Clothed in rough habits of brown wool, the nuns went wherever Francis and his monks went, practicing penance, rejoicing in God's wonderful world, and living on alms.

On her deathbed, Clare's last words were "Lord God, be blessed for having created me." This faithful nun, called by Francis his "little spiritual plant" outlived Francis by twenty-seven years, dying in 1253.

HER EMBLEM IN ART

Clare is usually represented in art holding a ciborium. This is from the time when Saracens came to plunder the city of Assisi. The terrified nuns ran to Clare who, carrying only the Blessed Sacrament, stood firmly before the attackers and confidently called upon God to protect her daughters and spare the city of Assisi. At the end of her prayer, she heard a voice say, "*Ego vos semper custodiam*" ("I will always protect you").

HER PATRONAGE

Clare is the patroness of embroidery workers, gilders, and washerwomen. She is invoked for good weather and against eye disease. Her protection is asked against all evils of the soul and body. Said to have taken part in Mass through a vision on her sickbed, Clare is the patron saint for television.

PRAYER FOR UNDERSTANDING

Blessed Clare, I come with a need for knowledge and understanding. I know that all things can work for good, and I ask that this may be revealed to me. Let me see the purpose of this burden so that I may bear it with willingness, with dignity, and with the knowledge that blessings will result from it.

Holy St. Clare, help me to perfect trust. Let me, like you, remember that God will always protect me.

St. Dymphna, Virgin, Martyr, Patroness for Mental Illness, Nervous and Emotional Disorders

The Belgian town of Gheel is unique. At any time you could find at least two thousand mentally ill people in residence there; anyone you meet may be a patient. These people are all welcome visitors in Gheel, taken into the homes of the townsfolk and cared for.

In the sixth century, a lovely Irish princess named Dymphna fled with her priest from her incestuous father, the pagan king of Oriel.

Dymphna was the king's only child. Her mother was a devout Christian of blameless character and extraordinary physical charms. The mother had Dymphna prepared for baptism, and a holy priest named Father Gerebernus made the king's daughter a child of God at the baptismal font.

While in her early teens, Dymphna vowed her virginity to Christ. She did not mention her vow to her father, however, for there was no telling how the pagan ruler would react if he knew his only child had no intentions of marrying and continuing the family.

After his wife's death, the king was advised to remarry. He vowed to marry no one less beautiful or kind than the wife he had lost. His wicked advisers proposed that Dymphna take her mother's place.

At first the king was horrified at this unnatural proposal. But the idea grew in his mind, and at last he manifested his evil designs to Dymphna. She asked for a month's delay, then went in haste to her confessor.

Father Gerebernus counseled her to seek safety in flight and he, along with the court jester and his wife, fled with the young princess to Gheel, a small town near Antwerp, Belgium.

The villagers gave them a kind reception, and they settled there as solitaries near the shrine dedicated to St. Martin of Tours.

The king nursed his fury at Dymphna's flight for a time, and then followed her trail of Irish money and caught up with her in the Belgian town. He attempted to persuade her to return with him, and when Father Gerebernus tried to speak up in her defense the king ordered his immediate death. When, in spite of his promises and his threats, Dymphna still refused to return with him, the king struck off her head with his sword. The young saint was barely fifteen years old.

The inhabitants of Gheel buried the two bodies simply in a cave in keeping with a prevalent custom. Soon the young maiden came to be regarded as a saint, a martyr of purity, and a champion over the wiles of the devil that had caused her father's madness. There was an ever-growing number of pilgrims. In the thirteenth century, when workmen removed the earth at the entrance to the cave to give the two a more appropriate burial, they were astonished to find two white tombs carved from a stone of a kind unknown in the neighborhood. On the girl's coffin they found a red tile bearing the words "Here lies the holy virgin and martyr Dymphna." This gave rise to a legend that the bodies had been interred by angels, since no one had recollection of the interment in white tombs.

A shrine of St. Dymphna was erected at Gheel and has drawn thousands of pilgrims through the centuries. Many miraculous cures have been reported here. One of the greatest miracles, however, is the caring, unterrified attitude of the citizens toward the poor disturbed folk who come there. This friendly acceptance may be one big factor in the many cures that are effected at the shrine.

The feast of St. Dymphna, the "Lily of Eire," is May 15. In the United States, devotion to this lovable girl saint is promoted by the Franciscan Mission Associates, who conduct a perpetual novena of prayer every Monday in the Franciscan seminaries. There is a national shrine chapel of St. Dymphna on the grounds of the Massillon Psychiatric Center at Massillon, Ohio.

This chapel was the first church in the U.S. to be dedicated to the saint in 1939. The shrine is the national headquarters for the League of St. Dymphna.

HER RELICS

During the Middle Ages, those who visited Gheel to invoke the saint were encouraged to make a nine-day devotion (novena) at the shrine, and many participated in seven ceremonies called penances. Among other practices, they were to recite prayers that were intended to exorcise the demons thought to cause the illness. Until the eighteenth century the same prayers were said in Gheel for all the sick, without any distinction between those believed devil-ridden and the mentally ill. During these prayers, the red stone found on the remains of St. Dymphna was hung around the necks of those afflicted. The weight of each patient was offered in wheat, which was sometimes substituted by the payment of thirty-two coins. Sometimes, depending on the resources of the person, the weight of the patient was offered to the saint in wine, silver, or gold in place of the customary wheat.*

The relics of the young saint are preserved today in a golden reliquary in a large church believed to be built over the site of her original burial.

Little St. Dymphna, although I am not mentally ill, I am sometimes despondent, tense, and nervous. These feelings give me an idea of the feelings of those who are suffering from mental illness. Be with me in my own times of stress, and through your prayers ask our Lord to grant his peace to the mentally ill.

_____

Note
* Cruz, *Relics* (Huntington, Ind., 1984), p. 239.

Opposite: St. Francis fresco by Cimabue (c.1240- c. 1302) at Assisi shows the saint's stigmata. Above: The crucifix that spoke to St. Francis, telling him to rebuild Christ's Church, an Umbrian cross with corpus painted in egg tempera, is also preserved at Assisi.

Francis of Assisi, Founder, Stigmatic, Patron of Ecology and Catholic Action

Francis of Assisi is one of the most popular of all saints. There is nothing more attractive than a happy person, and St. Francis was a happy person.

Until he was nineteen, Francis Bernardone was one of the rich playboys in the Italian town of Assisi. A severe illness gave him time to think, and he came out of it with more serious things on his mind. Francis was praying in the Church of San Damiano one day when he heard an image of the crucified Christ speak to him. "Go, Francis, and repair my house, which as you see is falling into ruin." Taking these words literally, Francis sold some of his father's goods and used the money to repair the church. Because of this, his father disinherited and disowned him. He gave up all claim to his family's wealth and went to live in a shack. He began to spend his time among the poor and the sick.

The happy personality that had made him a standout when he was a wealthy young man-about-town remained with him, and people flocked to hear him preach. Eleven of his boyhood friends left home and joined him in his poverty. Francis had discovered that all creation belongs to God. This made him brother to all of God's other creatures — people, animals, and birds. The world became one big family for Francis.

In 1210, Francis and his friends went to Rome to get the blessing of Pope Innocent III. This marks the beginning of the Franciscan order, which spread rapidly all over the world. In 1212, he founded, with St. Clare, the first community of Poor Ladies (now known as Poor Clares).

On September 17, 1224, Francis received the stigmata, the wounds of the Passion of Christ. He was the first recorded person in the history of the Church to be so honored. Francis died in Assisi in 1226 at the age of forty-four as he lay on the bare earth to signify his poverty and detachment from all things of the world.

THE STIGMATA

It is a well-authenticated fact that St. Francis of Assisi bore on his hands, feet, and side the marks of the Lord's five wounds of the crucifixion. In 1224, two years before his death, Francis had a vision in which he saw a cherub crucified and burning. It was at this time he received the stigmata. No case of the stigmata is known to have existed before the time of St. Francis, but over three hundred cases have been counted since. The stigmata of St. Francis were looked upon with wonder and described in detail by his companions. To date, science has no explanation of these marks.

HIS CANONIZATION

Francis, the Seraphic Father, was already addressed as "*il santo*" in his lifetime. Immediately following his death on October 3, 1226, the Franciscan Minister General Elias addressed a letter to Gregory of Naples and the Mendicants of France announcing the saint's death and the stigmata borne by him. These wounds were to represent the most visible sign of Francis' sainthood. After the general chapter of 1227, Elias requested Pope Gregory IX to canonize the Seraphic Father. He then secured a plot of land in Assisi on which a shrine was to be erected. By April 1228, the Pope issued the bull *Recolentes Qualiter* announcing the construction of a church and soliciting contributions. Thus, even prior to a canonization hearing, the decision had been made. A similar case of prejudgment marked the canonization of Clare of Assisi, foundress of the companion order of Poor Clares.[1]

HIS EMBLEM IN ART

St. Francis is depicted in art with the stigmata, and frequently with birds and animals.

HIS RELICS

Although he had requested that he be buried in the criminals' cemetery, the body of St. Francis was taken in solemn procession to the Church of St. George in Assisi, where it remained until 1230. Then it was secretly moved to the great basilica built by Brother Elias. Here it remained unseen until 1818, when it was relocated deep beneath the high altar in the lower church. Today, his remains recline in a triple urn atop an altar in a special chapel of the Basilica of St. Francis. In addition to his remains, the basilica has several other relics of the saint, including two of his habits. One is of rough gray cloth covered with patches, and the other, a white one, was made for him during his final illness by St. Clare herself. There is an autographed blessing of St. Francis written to Brother Leo, his confessor, which is displayed in a special reliquary framed with a trailing vine of golden roses.

The little chapel the saint restored, called the Portiuncula, stands today inside the great Church of St. Mary of the Angels. The cell in which the saint died is preserved under the bay of this basilica's choir.[2]

HIS PATRONAGE

Francis is the patron of merchants, of Italy, and of Catholic Action. A legendary champion of snared birds, beaten horses, and hungry dogs, he was named patron saint of ecologists by Pope John Paul II. He is invoked for the love of all persons and for when one is bored.

CUSTOMS

Our Christmas today reflects many of the ancient customs begun by St. Francis or connected with his devotion.

It was a widespread custom to be especially kind to animals at Christmas and to allow them to share in the joy of the feast. The custom was begun by St. Francis, who admonished the farmers to give their stock extra corn and hay at Christmas "for reverence of the Son of God, whom on such a night the blessed Virgin Mary did lay down in the stall between the ox and the ass." Francis believed that all creation should rejoice at Christmas, and the dumb creatures had no other means of doing so except by enjoying more comfort and better food.[3]

St. Francis was the first to introduce the joyous carol spirit which spread all over Europe. He wrote a beautiful Christmas hymn in Latin, and his companions and spiritual sons contributed a number of lovely Italian Christmas carols.[4]

The Child in the manger and various other graphic representations of the story of the Nativity have been used in church services from the first centuries. The crèche in its present form and use outside the church is credited to St. Francis, who made the Christmas crib popular through his famous celebration at Greccio, Italy, on Christmas Eve 1223, with a Bethlehem scene including live animals. Francis declared that he wanted to see with his own eyes "how poor and miserable He wished to be for our sake." At midnight, the brothers and the folk of the countryside came together, and Mass was said with the manger as an altar, so that the Divine Child under the forms of bread and wine should Himself come to the place. The saint, dressed in Deacon's vestments (Francis was never a priest), sang the Gospel and preached a delightful sermon.

It is said that a white flower grows beside the Basilica of St. Francis at Assisi and blooms, unreasonably, all year round.

TESTAMENT OF ST. FRANCIS OF ASSISI, CONFESSOR

We adore Thee, most holy Lord Jesus Christ, here and in all Thy churches that are in the whole world, and we bless Thee; because by Thy holy Cross Thou hast redeemed the world.

PRAYER FOR PEACE

Lord, make me an instrument of your peace.
Where there is hatred, let me sow love;
Where there is injury, pardon;
Where there is doubt, faith;
Where there is despair, hope;
Where there is darkness, light;
And where there is sadness, joy.
O Divine Master, grant that I may not so much seek to be
         consoled as to console,
To be understood as to understand,
To be loved as to love;
For it is in giving that we receive,
It is in pardoning that we are pardoned,
And it is in dying that we are born to eternal life.

[This anonymous "Prayer of St. Francis" was apparently not written by the saint, but it is imbued with his devotion, his sense of life-affirmation, and his gift for paradox.]

O Blessed St. Francis who lived in the greatest of poverty, help me to tear away from the world and its attachments to material things. Help me to live the spirit of poverty by putting my faith in Divine Providence instead of my own weak humanity.

Notes

1. Wilson, *Saints and Their Cults* (Cambridge, 1983), p. 176.

2. Cruz, *Relics* (Huntington, Ind., 1984), p. 180, 246.

3. Weiser, *Handbook of Christian Feasts and Customs* (New York, 1958), p. 74.

4. Ibid., p. 79.

St. George, Soldier, Patron of Boy Scouts and of England

Although it is agreed that George lived and died as a martyr, he is one of those "whose actions are only known to God," according to Pope Gelasius in 494. He was one of the most famous of the early martyrs, and his reputation is still alive, especially in the East, although no historical particulars of his life have survived. His legend has been so embroidered that earnest endeavors have been made to prove he never existed, but this is impossible to do. Veneration for St. George as a soldier saint was widespread from early times, and the center of his devotion was in Palestine at Diospolis, now Lydda. He was probably martyred there at the end of the third or the beginning of the fourth century.

In his legend, popularized in the later Middle Ages, he is represented as a knight from Cappadocia who was a victim of the persecution of Diocletian and was tortured and beheaded at Nicomedia for his faith.

The most famous legend about St. George is the story of how he killed the dragon. Back in his time (third century), it is said, there lived in a lake near the town of Silene in Libya a dragon so ferocious that the townspeople were kept in mortal terror. Every day the dragon would come to the city gates looking for food. For a while the people managed to stand him off by throwing out two sheep each day, but finally they had no more sheep and were reduced to giving him their children. One morning, St. George, an officer in the Roman army, came riding by the lake and found a beautiful maiden sitting there sobbing, waiting to be eaten. (There is no case on record of any dragon eating an ugly maiden.) The monster rose from the lake and started for his breakfast, but St. George held him at bay with his lance and instructed the girl to put her belt around the dragon's neck. They led the venomous beast back to the town, and inside the city walls George struck off its head and lifted the terrible siege. George told the people it was the power of Christ which made him able to save them, and the entire populace was converted.

The fact that there is no such thing as a dragon has never hurt this legend, nor has anyone apparently been bothered about the mathematics of the staggering reported number of baptisms at Silene. Twenty thousand baptisms in one day would mean thirteen per minute for a full twenty-four hours. The origin of this fanciful tale is impossible to determine, but it was accepted and carried in the missals and breviaries of the Church until Pope Clement VII, in the sixteenth century, caused it to be dropped.[1]

How St. George came to be adopted as the protector of England is not clear. His name was known in England and Ireland long before the Norman conquest, and it is probable that returning Crusaders did much to establish his popularity. King Richard the First (the Lion-Hearted) named him the special patron of the Crusaders, and later this patronage was extended to all knights and to soldiers in general. A synod at Oxford in 1222 declared him the patron of England. The Order of the Garter was established under his patronage by King Edward III in 1348. In 1970, the annual feast of the saint in Roman Catholic churches was made optional.

HIS EMBLEM IN ART

In art, St. George is depicted with a dragon.

PATRONAGES

St. George is the patron of England, soldiers, Boy Scouts, and the titular saint of numerous churches throughout the world. He is a patron of cavalry, horses, blacksmiths, and

*Van der Weyden miniature showing St. George in medieval armor is
only slightly larger than this at the National Gallery, Washington.*

St. George medal for scouting worn by airman (U.S. Air Force photo).

farmers. He is also the patron saint for mentally retarded persons. St. George is called upon to help alleviate the problem of skin diseases such as eczema and psoriasis. His aid is invoked to conquer fear, and to give courage and humility.

CUSTOMS

Among the South Slavonians, a barren woman who desired a child placed a new chemise on a fruitful tree on the eve of St. George's Day. Next morning before sunrise she examined the garment, and if she found that some living creature had crept on it she could hope that her wish would be fulfilled within the year. Then she put on the chemise confident that she would be as fruitful as the tree.[2] In Ukraine on St. George's Day (April 23), the priest in his robes, attended by acolytes, went out to the fields where crops were beginning to show green and blessed them. After that the young married people lay down in couples on the fields and rolled on them to promote the growth of crops. In some parts of Russia the priest himself was rolled over the crops.[3]

In medieval mystery plays, St. George was represented killing the dragon. The actor playing the saint's part made certain his spear pierced a bag filled with "blood" attached to the inside of the dragon's skin, making the red liquid flow copiously while the monster "died" to the great delight of the spectators.

In the legendary folklore of the Middle Ages, St. George had the task of driving demons and witches away from the homes and fields. Much of this lore survived in parts of Europe to our own century. In Germany and Austria, boys cracked whips on the eve of his feast to help the saint drive demons away. In Poland, farmers lit fires in their yards to frighten evil spirits away. On the morning of the feast, the dew was mixed into the fodder to make the animals immune to attacks of demons or witches. Polish farmers have a fairy tale that St. George lives in the moon, which the Blessed Mother gave him as a reward for his great deeds. From there he comes down on his feast day with a "key" to open the earth and free plants and flowers from the shackles of winter.

In Alpine countries and among the Slavic nations, it was customary to drive domestic animals to spring pastures on St. George's Day. Farm hands blew merrily on their trumpets (*Georgiblasen*) while they marched with the cattle out into the open. In Austria, it was a tradition to take a spring hike through the countryside on the saint's feast.[4]

St. George is the most popular saint in philately, honored on more stamps by more countries than any other saint. In most of the stamp designs, he is shown on horseback in battle with the dragon.[5]

St. George, help me to be a good soldier for Christ, and to slay the dragons of temptation and fear.

Notes

1. Harper, *Days and Customs of All Faiths* (New York, 1957), p. 99.

2. Frazer, *The Golden Bough* (New York, 1940), pp. 119-120.

3. Ibid., p. 137.

4. Weiser, *The Holyday Book*, p. 160-163.

5. Patrick R. Moran, ed., *Day by Day With the Saints* (Huntington, Ind., 1985), p. 81.

St. John the Baptizer, Prophet, Cousin of Jesus, Patron of Missionaries and Farriers

St. John the Baptizer (or Baptist), as the forerunner of Jesus, has always occupied a high place in Christianity. In the Eastern Church, devotion to him is second only to the Blessed Virgin Mary. He was highly honored throughout the whole Church from the beginning. Christ's high praise (Matthew 11:11) encouraged a special veneration.

St. John's principal feast day, contrary to the usual custom, is kept on the anniversary of his birth, June 24, rather than his death. Other saints' days are celebrated on the day of their death when their final victory is won. St. John's is celebrated at his birth, as there was a strong belief among the faithful that John was freed from original sin at the moment when his mother met the Blessed Virgin (Luke 1:41). John's is one of the oldest feasts in the liturgy of the Church, having been celebrated continuously since the fourth century. In earlier times it ranked among the most joyous feasts of the year. His death by beheading is also observed on August 29.

John's parents were a priest of Jerusalem, Zechariah or Zachary, and Elizabeth, a kinswoman of the Virgin Mary. His birth in their old age was foretold by the angel Gabriel. He was born six months before Jesus.

As an adult, John lived as a hermit in the desert of Judea. There is a good possibility that John spent some time with the Essene community, whose documents and buildings have been studied at Qumran near the Dead Sea since 1947.[1]

About the year 27, John appeared as an itinerant preacher. He announced, "Repent, for the Kingdom of Heaven is at hand." All who confessed their sins were washed in the river Jordan. John gained many followers, including several who were later chosen as apostles of Christ. Jesus came Himself to be baptized by John; here, John pointed to Jesus as "the Lamb of God who takes away the sins of the world." (Cf. John 1:29-36.)

Soon after Jesus' baptism, John was thrown into prison because he had rebuked Herod Antipas for marrying Herodias, his half-brother's wife. From prison he followed Jesus' ministry and sent messengers to ask Him questions. In a moment of folly, Herod promised to give Salome, Herodias's daughter, whatever she wanted. The girl's mother told her to ask for John the Baptist's head. Her request was honored, and John went to his death silently and helplessly. His death occurred about a year before our Lord's.

HIS RELICS

In the fifteenth century, an important pilgrimage to St. John's shrine at Traoun-Meriadek in Brittany arose. This was encouraged by the dukes and centered on the claim of the shrine to possess the Baptist's index finger.[2]

HIS PATRONAGE

John is the patron saint of missionaries because he was sent to prepare the way of the Lord. He is also considered the patron of farriers (blacksmiths).

SWEETHEARTS OF ST. JOHN

In Sardinia there was a great midsummer festival that bore the name of St. John the Baptist. At the end of March or on the first of April, a young man of the village presented himself to a girl and asked her to be his *comare* (sweetheart), offering to be her *compare*. The invitation was considered an honor by her family and was gladly accepted. At the end of May the girl made a pot out of the bark of the cork-tree, filling it with earth and sowing a handful of wheat and barley in it. The pot was placed in the sun and watered, so the plant had a good head by St. John's Eve (June 23 — also called Midsummer's Eve). The pot was then called Erme or Nenneri. On St. John's Day, the young man and the girl, dressed in their best and accompanied by a large retinue, walked in procession to the local church. Here they threw the pot against the door of the church, after which they sat and ate eggs and herbs to the music of flutes. Wine was mixed in a cup and passed round, each one drinking as it passed. Then all joined hands and sang "Sweethearts of St. John," over and over again after which they finished the evening with a dance. This was the general custom in Sardinia. As practiced at Ozieri, on the eve of the feast, the window sills were draped with rich cloths on which the pots were placed, gaily adorned with red and blue silk and varicolored ribbons. Each pot held a statuette or cloth doll dressed as a woman or a priapic male figure. This custom was rigorously forbidden by the Church. The boys walked about together to look at the pots and then waited for the girls who assembled on the public square for the festival. Here they kindled a great bonfire. Those who wished to be "Sweethearts of St. John" grasped the ends of a long stick which they then passed through the fire to seal their relationship to each other.

Similar customs were observed at the same time in Sicily. Pairs of boys and girls became gossips (sweethearts) of St. John on St. John's Day by each drawing a hair from his or her head and performing various ceremonies over them. They tied the hairs together and threw them up in the air or exchanged them over a potsherd which they afterwards broke in two, with each person preserving a fragment with pious care. The tie formed in this way was supposed to last for life. In some parts of Sicily the gossips of St. John presented each other with plates of sprouting corn, lentils, and canary seed which had been planted forty days before the festival. The one who received the plate pulled a stalk of the young plants, bound it with a ribbon and preserved it among his or her greatest treasures, restoring the platter to the giver. At Catania, the gossips exchanged pots of basil and great cucumbers. The girls tended the basil, and the thicker it grew the more it was prized. In these midsummer customs of Sicily and Sardinia, it is possible that St. John has replaced the pagan Adonis with ancient fertility rites.[3] Basil and garlic were also important plants in the Baptist's cult in Portugal.

ST. JOHN'S FIRES

Fire festivals were generally held all over Europe during the summer solstice, on Midsummer Eve (June 23) or Midsummer Day (June 24). A tinge of Christianity was given to them by naming Midsummer Day after St. John the Baptist, but there is no doubt that the celebration dates from a time long before the Christian era. The Lord had once called John the Baptist a lamp "set aflame and burning bright," (John 5:35), and the Church insisted that this was the real symbolism of the fires. What happened, however, was that St. John the Baptist was let in on the superstitions and began to be invoked along with the bonfires against the misfortunes the fires were supposed to prevent.

A writer from the first half of the sixteenth century wrote that in almost every village and town of Germany public bonfires were kindled on the Eve of St. John and young and old of both sexes gathered about them, passing the time in dancing and singing. The people wore chaplets of mugwort and vervain and looked at the fire through bunches of larkspur they held in their hands, believing that this would preserve their eyes in a healthy state throughout the year. They concluded by throwing the mugwort and vervain into the fire to burn up their bad luck. The fires were connected to the harvest; around Baden, the people jumped over the fires to prevent backache at the time of harvest.

In Norway, the fires were said to banish both sickness and witches. In Sweden, the Eve of St. John was the most joyous night of the whole year. It was celebrated by the frequent discharge of firearms as well as the bonfires. Here the festival was one of water as well as of fire, and certain holy springs were then supposed to be endowed with wonderful medicinal values. In the lower valley of the Inn, an effigy called the Lotter, apparently a corruption of "Luther," was carried about the village and then burned. At Ambras, one of the villages where Martin Luther was thus burned in effigy, they said that if you went through the village between eleven and twelve on St. John's Night and washed yourself in three wells, you would see all who were to die in the following year. The Estonians believed that the St. John's fire kept witches from the cattle and said that he who did not come to the bonfire would have thistles and weeds in his harvest.

In Brittany, the custom of the midsummer bonfires was kept up to the middle of this century. Here they had a slightly more Christian ritual associated with them. When the flames died down, the whole assembly knelt round the bonfire and an old man prayed aloud. Then all rose and marched thrice around the fire; at the third turn they all stopped, picked up a pebble, and threw it on the burning fire.

At Jumièges in Normandy, down to the first half of the nineteenth century, the festival was marked by certain singular features which bore the stamp of antiquity. Every year the Brotherhood of the Green Wolf chose a new chief or master. The new head assumed the title of the Green Wolf and donned a peculiar costume consisting of a long green mantle and a very tall green hat of a conical shape and without a brim. Thus arrayed, he stalked solemnly at the head of the brothers, chanting the hymn of St. John, with crucifix and holy banner leading the way to a place called Chouquet. Here the procession was met by the priest, precentors, and choir, who conducted the brotherhood to the parish church. After hearing Mass the company adjourned to the house of the Green Wolf, where a simple meal was served. At night, a bonfire was kindled to the sound of handbells rung by a young man and woman decked with flowers. Then the Green Wolf and his brothers, with hoods down on their shoulders and holding each other by the hand, ran round the fire after the man chosen to be the Green Wolf of the following year. Though only the first and last man in the chain had a free hand, they made three attempts to seize the future Green Wolf, who in his efforts to escape hit the brothers with a long wand he carried. When they finally caught him, they carried him to the burning pile and pretended to throw him on it. After this ceremony, they returned to the house of the Green Wolf, where another simple supper was set out. Up till midnight a sort of religious solemnity prevailed, but at the stroke of midnight this was changed. Constraint gave way to license; pious hymns were replaced by bacchanalian ditties, and the shrill, quivering notes of the village fiddle hardly rose above the roar of voices of the merry brotherhood of the Green Wolf. The celebration continued the next day. One of the ceremonies consisted in parading an enormous loaf of blessed bread which rose in tiers and was surmounted by a pyramid of verdure adorned with ribbons. After that the old handbells, deposited on the steps of the altar, were entrusted as insignia of office to the man who was to be the Green Wolf the next year.[4]

THE OIL OF ST. JOHN

On St. John's morning, the peasants of Piedmont and Lombardy went out to search the oak leaves for the "oil of St. John," which was supposed to heal all wounds made with cutting instruments. Originally, perhaps, this oil was simply mistletoe or a decoction made from it. In the French province

Baptism of Jesus by Andrea del Sarto (1486-1530), a detail from a series of frescoes on the life of St. John the Baptist in Florence, Italy.

*Salome with the head of John the Baptist, detail from a diptych by
Hans Memling (1433-94) at St. John's Hospital in Bruges, Belgium.*

of Bourbonnais, a popular remedy for epilepsy was a decoction of mistletoe that had been gathered on an oak on St. John's Day and boiled with rye flour.[5]

OTHER CUSTOMS

In some parts of Southern and Western Russia, the women, without stripping off their clothes, bathed in crowds on the feast day of St. John the Baptist in order to insure rain. While bathing, they dipped in the water a figure made of branches, grass, and herbs which was supposed to represent the saint.[6]

In Athens, Greece, there was a little chapel of St. John the Baptist built against an ancient column. Fever patients went there and attached a waxed thread to the inner side of the column. In this manner, they believed, they transferred the fever from themselves to the pillar.[7]

St. John Baptist, help me remember and honor the vows made for me at my baptism. As you did with words, let me by my actions announce the Lord Jesus Christ.

Notes

1. Attwater, *Avenel Dictionary of Saints* (New York, 1981), p. 191.

2. Wilson, ed., *Saints and Their Cults* (Cambridge, 1983), p. 7.

3. Frazer, *The Golden Bough* (New York, 1940), pp. 524-531.

4. Ibid., p. 624-631.

5. Ibid., p. 663.

6. Ibid., p. 70.

7. Ibid., p. 545.

St. Jude Thaddeus, Apostle, Patron of Hopeless Cases

The origins of devotion to St. Jude as patron of difficult or hopeless cases are nearly as obscure as details of the life of the great apostle. There seems to have been a spontaneous rising of interest among the faithful themselves, possibly prompted by the fact that according to tradition St. Jude was a near relative of Jesus, and that as a child he was a playmate of the Lord. The Gospel tells us that St. Jude was a brother of James the Less, also one of the apostles.

Because of confusion of the names of the saint and the traitor Judas, devotion to the saint was effectively discouraged for many centuries. The devotion began to be popular during the Middle Ages. Our Lord himself directed St. Bridget of Sweden to turn to St. Jude with great confidence.

Tradition tells that St. Jude's father, Alphaeus, was murdered because of his outspoken devotion to the risen Christ. The mother of St. Jude and St. James the Less, also named Mary, was a cousin of the Virgin Mary. Miracles were attributed to her intercession after her death.

Legends of the Apostle Jude are tied in with the story of the Shroud of Turin. King Abgar of the city of Edessa in northwestern Mesopotamia, about 350 miles north of Galilee, was stricken with a dread disease, probably leprosy. He had heard of Jesus and His healing miracles, and sent a message begging Jesus to cure him. When the message arrived, Jesus had already ascended into Heaven. The apostles, impressed with the king's faith, decided to send Jude with the Holy Shroud. It could not be brought and shown as a shroud because all people have a natural revulsion toward objects which have been in close contact with the dead. Before being brought to the king, therefore, the cloth seems to have been folded and decorated so that it showed only the portrait-like image of the

Holy Face of Jesus. Jude brought the shroud to Edessa, and the king was cured and baptized. Jude then established Christianity in Edessa.[1]

St. Jude reportedly traveled through Mesopotamia for ten years preaching and evangelizing. With St. Simon (the Zealot), he later visited Libya and Persia to convert the people there.

According to tradition, St. Jude died a martyr's death. He was clubbed, and his head was then shattered with a broad ax. Later his body was brought to Rome and placed in a crypt in an honored position in the left transept of St. Peter's Basilica.

ST. JUDE'S HOSPITAL

One person who experienced the effect of St. Jude's patronage was Catholic entertainer Danny Thomas. As a young comedian in Detroit, he found himself one day without a job, with a pregnant wife, and nearly flat broke. Sitting in a church pondering whether to quit show business and get some sort of menial job in order to pay the bills, he saw a pamphlet about St. Jude. He asked himself what case could be more hopeless than his own. He put his last seven dollars in the prayer box, asking the saint to return his money tenfold. On his return home, there was a message asking him to do a radio commercial for a fee of seventy-five dollars, five dollars more than he had asked for.

In 1943, Thomas asked St. Jude's help in making a big decision. He promised that if the saint would give him a sign, he would build a shrine where the poor, helpless, and homeless could come for comfort and aid. He received his sign that night; again his prayers were answered.

Two years later in Chicago, Thomas remembered the vow he had made. He got the idea for a hospital where children would be cared for regardless of race, creed, or the ability to pay; a place where no suffering child would be refused. He talked to his friends about his idea, then formed a committee and a board of directors. They decided the hospital would care for children with catastrophic, often fatal diseases. It would be devoted to research and would share the benefits of its knowledge with medical facilities worldwide.

St. Jude's hospital opened February 4, 1962, in Memphis, Tennessee. Today, the hospital offers care to over 3,500 sick children and has increased the survival rate for childhood cancers from less than five percent to over sixty percent.

HIS RELICS AND SHRINES

The major relics of this saint are enshrined in St. Peter's Basilica in Rome. Small relics have been distributed worldwide, but a major relic, the forearm, is kept at the St. Jude Shrine in Chicago. This relic is kept in a silver reliquary shaped as a life-size forearm. A glass section exposes the relic to view.[2] Another major shrine in the U.S. dedicated to the saint is in Baltimore, Maryland. St. Jude is the titular patron for many churches in this country, many of which have a shrine in his honor.

HIS EMBLEM IN ART

St. Jude is pictured with a square rule, carrying the image of Jesus on a disc in his hand, carrying a staff, club, or sword, and with a flame over his head.

HIS PATRONAGE

St. Jude is possibly one of the most popular of all saints, for he is known as the saint of the impossible and hopeless causes.

NEWSPAPER ADS AND CHAIN LETTERS

Two customs which border on superstitious practice rather than true piety have been popularized in connection with the devotion to St. Jude.

A familiar sight in the classified-ad section of the daily newspaper is a short prayer to the patron saint of difficult or hopeless cases. The ad may be a brief thank-you, or it may be a complete prayer with detailed instructions to readers on how to go about this form of devotional worship. Although such published prayers incorporate several aspects which are in the mainstream of Catholic devotions such as intercessory prayer and novenas, the reader is often told he must promise publication when starting the novena and publish immediately when the prayer is answered. The ads also frequently tell the reader the devotion has never been known to fail. Although many persons who practice this form of devotion are undoubtedly sincere, the ads smack of playing games with God. They represent a misguided faith which attempts to manipulate God.

Within the past two years, the author of this book has received no fewer than four copies of a chain letter purportedly part of a devotion connected with St. Jude. All copies have been sent anonymously. The letter announces that it has been sent for good luck which will occur within four days of its receipt provided the receiver sends it on. The letter demands that twenty copies be sent. The mention of the great benefits which have come to those who mailed it on, and the drastic problems, including death, experienced by those who failed to continue the chain, make the letter simply superstition and spiritual blackmail.

PRAYER IN A DESPERATE SITUATION

O God, through your Blessed St. Jude, I pray for help in my extreme need. The despair I feel has blocked out all hope, all confidence, all faith in a just solution to this situation. Bring to me a spirit of trust and an optimistic attitude which will bring about an improvement of my circumstances. You know all my needs and so I pray for speedy assistance, along with a restoration of my knowledge that all things work for good when trust in your mercy is placed above all other thoughts.

Blessed St. Jude, cousin of our Lord, help me to imitate your fidelity to God's call. By your powerful intercession, please help me in my pressing needs, and keep me faithful to Christ.

Notes

1. Anne Carroll, *Christ the King: Lord of History* (Manassas, Va., 1986), p. 83.

2. Cruz, *Relics* (Huntington, Ind., 1984), p. 114.

St. Margaret, Shepherdess, Patron of Women in Childbirth

Margaret, a third-century virgin martyr, was one of the most popular saints in the later Middle Ages in the West. There is, however, no positive evidence about her, and much of her story is a fictitious romance. In the East, she is called Marina.

Considered the epitome of feminine meekness and innocence, Margaret was a girl of striking beauty, the daughter of a pagan priest of Antioch. She was converted to Christianity by her nurse, and her father would have nothing more to do with her. He drove her from her home, and she took up the life of a shepherdess for her support. Here she was seen by Olybrius, governor of Antioch, who was smitten with her beauty and who wanted to marry her at once. She declined saying she was committed to Christ. In his wounded pride, the governor had her thrown into a dungeon.

Margaret's legend tells that Satan appeared to her in the dungeon in the form of a dragon and swallowed her. Inside of him, she made the sign of the cross, and he disgorged her intact. The story continues that she prayed that she might be of help in all precarious deliveries, and in this way she became the patron saint of all women in childbirth. After her imprisonment, the governor had her tortured and beheaded.

HER EMBLEM IN ART

In art, Margaret is usually portrayed with a dragon.

HER PATRONAGES

Margaret is called on by expectant mothers and those in childbirth.

CUSTOMS

In medieval Poitou, reading a saint's life aloud was considered to be a kind of prayer. To facilitate a woman in labor, the Life of St. Margaret was chosen.[1]

In a prayer to St. Margaret, "folken alle that be disconsolat, / In your myschief and grete adversite, / And alle that stone of helpe desolate," were invited to pray to the saint for relief.

By the seventeenth century in most European countries, mystery plays were performed after a procession to a public square or church in honor of the feast of Corpus Christi. St. George, St. Margaret, and their dragons were among the most popular characters of these pageants and processions, manifestations of baroque piety.[2]

Holy Margaret, just as you broke loose from the dragon by the sign of the cross, help me escape the dragons of sin and complacence with the cross as my guide.

Notes

1. Wilson, *Saints and Their Cults* (Cambridge, 1983), p. 16.
2. Weiser, *Handbook of Christian Feasts and Customs* (New York, 1958), p. 264.

St. Jude Thaddeus (San Judas Tadeo) in a fragrant Mexican picture taken from a pack of incense sold to invoke the saint's intercession.

WITH LOVE ALL THINGS ARE POSSIBLE

This paper has been sent to you for good luck. The original is
in New England. It has been around the world nine times. The
luck has now been sent to you. You will receive good luck within
four days of receiving this letter, provided you, in turn, send
it on.

This is no joke. You will receive good luck in the mail. Send
no money. Send copies to people you wish to have good luck.
Send no money as fate has no price. Do not keep this letter. It
must leave your hands within 96 hours.

AN R.A.V OFFICER RECEIVED $170,000.00

Joe Elliot received $40,000.00 and lost it because he broke the
chain.

While in the Philippines, Gene Welch lost his wife six days after
receiving the letter. He had failed to circulate it. However,
before her death he received $7,755,000.00.

Please send 20 copies and see what happens in four days. The
chain comes from Venezuela and was written by Saul Anthony
Degroup, a missionary from South America. Since the copy must
tour the world, you must make 20 copies and send them to friends
and associates. After a few days, you will get a surprise. THIS
IS TRUE, even if you are not superstitious.

Please note the following: Constantine Dias received the chain
in 1953. He asked his secretary to make 20 copies and send them
out. A few days later he won a lottery prize of two million
dollars. Carlos Daditt, an office employee, received and letter
and forgot it had to leave his hands within 96 hours. He lost
his job. Later, after finding the letter again, he mailed 20
copies. A few days later, he got a better job. Dalan Fairchild
received the letter and, not believing it, threw the letter away.
Nine days later, he died.

In 1987, the letter, received by a young woman in California, had
become very faded and barely readable. She promised herself that
she would retype the letter and send it on, but she put it aside
to redo later. She was plagued with various problems including
expensive car repairs. The letter did not leave her hands in 96
hours. She finally typed the letter, as promised, and got a new
car.

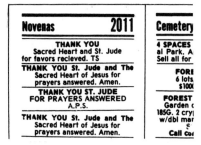

*Top: St. Jude superstitions include chain letters threatening disasters.
Below: Typical "thank-you" classified ads from the Houston Post.*

St. Martin of Tours, Bishop, Patron of Soldiers and Peacemakers

St. Martin was born at Sabaria, in what is now Hungary, about 316, the son of a pagan soldier. He entered the Roman army at the age of fifteen and served for twenty years.

Martin was a good officer. He lived frugally and often gave the remainder of his pay to charity. In 337, Martin was stationed at Amiens, where he had a vision of Christ. Passing through the city one winter morning, he spied a beggar leaning against the city wall. Martin had no money with him, so he tore his cloak in half and gave it to the beggar with a word of encouragement. That night in a happy dream, Martin saw a vision of Heaven. In the midst of the Celestial Hosts stood the Savior, wrapped in a soldier's torn cloak. Soon after this, Martin openly declared himself a Christian and requested baptism. He left the army and became a monk under St. Hilary at Poitiers.

At Poitiers, Martin practiced many charitable works, attempting to alleviate the poverty and suffering of his people. He and St. Hilary began to preach against the Arian heresy. Both were exiled for a time because of their opposition to Arianism, unable to return until 360. Martin spent the time living as a hermit.

Finally, Martin heard that St. Hilary was returning to Poitiers and followed him, hoping to continue the life of a hermit at some place near his friend. It is believed that he established the first monastic community in France at Ligugé about this time, thus predating St. Benedict as a father of monasticism in the West.

Over his protests, Martin was elected Bishop of Tours in 371. Martin preferred simplicity and did not live the indulgent lifestyle that many bishops of his time adopted. He was uncomfortable living in the city, so he retired to a place in the desert close by, establishing the monastery of Marmoutier. From here he carried out the duties of his office, traveling throughout western France.

On seeing a shorn sheep he said, "This sheep teaches a lesson from the Gospel. She gave one of her coats to someone who had none." There are many stories that tell of Martin giving away his own clothing to the poor, showing that he kept that Gospel lesson well himself.

Martin was sometimes plagued by the devil, who appeared to him in varying forms, often as pagan gods or goddesses. He drove away their temptations with prayer and the sign of the cross. This is possibly the root of his patronage against impure thoughts.

St. Martin was an extremely active missionary. His preaching was reinforced by his reputation as a wonder-worker. He traveled to the remotest parts of his diocese by foot, by donkey, and by water.

As an evangelizer of rural Gaul and the father of monasticism in France, St. Martin of Tours was a figure of great importance. His fame spread far and wide, and his influence was felt from Ireland to Africa and the East. St. Martin was one of the first holy men who was not a martyr to be publicly venerated as a saint.

In 384, St. Ambrose and Martin opposed Ithacius, the Bishop of Ossanova. He wanted a notorious heretic, Priscillian, put to death, but Ambrose and Martin would not hear of it. Eventually Emperor Maximus had the heretic killed. In order to prevent further bloodshed, Martin reached a compromise with Ithacius but remained troubled by his decision.

Martin fell ill in a remote part of his diocese. When someone suggested he turn on his side to relieve his discomfort, he responded, "Let me look toward Heaven rather than earth so that my soul may journey on the right course to the Lord."

Martin died November 8, 397.

HIS IMAGE IN ART

In art, St. Martin is usually portrayed as a Roman soldier astride a fine horse. He is shown using a sword to cut his cloak in half to present to a beggar in commemoration of his conversion experience. In Spanish, he is known as San Martín del Caballo (St. Martin of the Horse) or Caballero (Knight). In some old pictures of St. Martin there is a rabbit painted at his feet. This is in remembrance of one of his miracles of mercy wherein he is said to have rescued the poor creature from the dogs of hunters. He is also sometimes depicted with a vanquished demon at his feet.

HIS PATRONAGE

Martin is the patron of soldiers and of conscientious objectors or peacemakers. He is also one of the patrons of France, of tavern keepers, of beggars, of winegrowers, and of drunkards, both practicing and reformed.

CUSTOMS

The most common and almost universal harvest and thanksgiving celebration held in medieval times was on the Feast of St. Martin, Martinmas, on November 11. It was a holiday in Germany, France, Holland, England, and central Europe. After Mass, the rest of the day was filled with games, dances, parades, and a festive dinner. The main feature of the meal was Martin's goose, a traditional roast goose. St. Martin's wine, the first lot of wine made from the grapes of the recent harvest, was drunk with dinner. Martinmas was the festival which commemorated the filled barns and stocked larders. Martinmas is still kept in some rural sections of Europe.[1]

The celebration of Christ's nativity on December 25 was

introduced as a special feast in Rome about the middle of the fourth century and it quickly spread throughout the Roman empire. As it was one of the main feasts, a spiritual preparation soon began to be held. A definite period for this preparation was first prescribed in Gaul about 490 by Bishop Perpetuus of Tours, who ruled a fast should be held on three days of every week from the Feast of St. Martin (November 11) to Christmas. The name advent was not yet used; it was called *Quadragesima Sancti Martini*, or Forty Days' Fast of St. Martin.

The name St. Martin's summer came into use to describe a short period of fine, summery weather in the fall about the time of Martinmas (Indian summer).[2]

In life, Martin effected a number of cures of the sick. It has been pointed out that therapy by exorcism, such as that practiced by him, was a form of the classical treatment by evacuation.[3] Some customs which arose in different areas had much of the magical element in them, however, rather than the devotional or medical. For instance, pilgrims to a statue of St. Martin in the Church of Crossville-la-Vieille (Eure), which was supposed to cure stomach disorders, brought two ribbons with them, one of which was left hanging on the statue while the other, having also touched the saint, was worn for nine days, then burned and its ashes buried in the ground.

Even today, among the Spanish-speaking who have a great devotion to San Martin, there are remnants of these magical elements connected to the devotion. In a Mexican yerbaria, for instance, you can find a variety of perfumes, incenses, and waters labeled with the saint's name. Wondrous properties are claimed for these. One bottle in the author's possession is labeled in Spanish as "sanctified sprinkling water of San Martín de Caballero." The directions note, "on finishing your bath or cleaning, apply to the body, to the house, the place of business, the automobile, etc." Sprinkling this water is supposed to bring wealth and good luck.

ST. MARTIN'S GOOSE

Martinmas is a day rich in tradition in Europe. One essential to the proper observance of his day is roast goose for dinner. Probably this is because geese are fat and plentiful at this time, but legend gives a more colorful reason. The story is that when Martin heard in 374 that he had been elected Bishop of Tours he was so horrified that he ran and hid in a barn. A stupid, meddlesome goose found him there and set up a racket that led the searchers to his hiding place. Descendants of the goose are still paying for this disservice.

THE HUMILIATION OF HIS RELICS

Monastic communities performed two religious functions vital to medieval society. First, the religious prayed for the salvation and well-being of the local population both living and dead. This was a vital concern to a population obsessed with the insecurity of this life and the uncertainly of the next. Second, through the Divine Office, the Mass, and the cult of the saints whose relics were honored in the community's church, they fulfilled the ritual actions necessary to keep the spiritual powers benevolently disposed toward human society. The relationship between the saint and the community who venerated his relics or body was reciprocal; the saint was a powerful protector for the community. In order to force cooperation or fair dealing, the monks manipulated their "salvific" function by ceasing to pray for or by cursing their opponents. Through the ritual of the clamor (*clamour*) and the accompanying humiliation of relics and images, they mistreated cult objects and prevented popular access to them, thus disturbing the proper relationships between the human and the supernatural orders and involving not only the alleged opponent but all of society which depended on these powers.

The clamor and the humiliation are closely related and

appear in a variety of combinations in liturgical manuscripts from the tenth until the thirteenth century. One ritual of humiliation that has been preserved is that liturgy as practiced at St. Martin of Tours.

After Prime, when all the bells of the tower had been rung, the canons entered the choir. They sang seven psalms and a litany. The most important members of the community and the ministers then placed on the ground a silver crucifix and all of the reliquaries of the saints, and put thorns on top of and all around the tomb of St. Martin. In the center of the nave, they placed a wooden crucifix, likewise covered with thorns, and they blocked all but one of the church doors with thorns. At dawn, the office of the day began in a subdued tone. Everything was muted, and the Mass of the day was celebrated as though it were a private Mass. The canons joined the relics on the floor before the Eucharist. The prayers and psalms sung during the rite explained the situation, the nature of the injustice, and articulated the necessary conclusion of the affair. The main prayers were drawn from the rich psalm literature of cries to the Lord in times of oppression. A few members of the laity were admitted to the church to observe the humiliation. The relics remained humiliated until a successful conclusion to the affair was reached.

In late 996 or early 997, Count Fulk Nerra of Anjou and Touraine entered the cloister of St. Martin of Tours with armed soldiers and damaged the house of the treasurer. The canons saw this as an atrocity, as the monastery was supposed to be immune from the count's jurisdiction. Therefore, they humiliated the relics of their saints. In addition to covering the relics with thorns, they kept the doors of the church closed day and night, refusing admission to the count or any of the members of his castle. At least five of the count's ancestors were buried in the monastery so he thus had no access to their tombs either. At last he softened.

The count, regretting his actions and seeking forgiveness, entered the cloister. He walked barefoot into the church with some of his followers. Stopping first before the sepulchre of Blessed Martin, he promised God and the saint he would never do such a thing again. In turn, he went to each humbled sacred object, asking forgiveness and humbling himself. Subsequently, the relics were returned to their place of honor and good relations were reestablished between the count and the monastery.

The humiliation of relics was often effective, although sometimes the crimes of the "oppressors" of the monastery were not grave ones. By the end of the thirteenth century, the episcopal and papal hierarchy were becoming increasingly unhappy with the tendency of communities to humiliate their relics and to discontinue services without canonical grounds. The Second Council of Lyon, in 1274, condemned humiliation as an arbitrary cessation of the liturgy, terming it a "detestable abuse of horrendous indevotion."[4]

PRAYER AGAINST IMPURE THOUGHTS

With trust and faith I beg you, Blessed St. Martin, to defend me against impure and evil thoughts which may stain my soul and come to thwart my desire for the true and complete satisfaction which is offered through perfect love. Rescue me from the mire lest I sink. Let not the deep swallow me up. Your mercy is great; draw near to me and lift me up, I pray.

Blessed St. Martin, help me imitate your holy charity in giving of my own worldly goods to the poor and the homeless.

Notes

1. Weiser, *Handbook of Christian Feasts and Customs* (New York, 1958), p.270.

2. Ibid., p. 49.

3. Wilson, op. cit., p. 20.

4. Ibid., pp. 125-139.

St. Michael, Archangel, Patron of Holy Souls, Soldiers, Policemen, Firemen

St. Michael the archangel is one of three angels named in Holy Scripture. Christian tradition assigns four offices to him: (1) to fight against Satan, (2) to rescue the souls of the faithful from the power of the devil, especially at the hour of death, (3) to be the champion of God's people, and (4) to call away from earth and bring men's souls to judgment. He was venerated from earliest Christian times as an angelic healer. There is evidence for the honor in which he was held from the beginnings of Christian history, and he was also venerated by the Jews.

St. Michael's feast was originally combined with the remembrance of all angels, and had been celebrated in Rome from the early centuries. In 813, it was introduced in all the countries of the Carolingian Empire and was celebrated as a public holiday. All through medieval times, St. Michael's Day was kept as a great religious feast and one of the annual holiday seasons as well. Two apparitions of the Archangel, at Mont-Saint-Michel (France) and on Mount Gargano (Italy) at one time had special feast days assigned to commemorate them. From the early centuries it was a favorite practice in the Oriental Church to build shrines to the saint on the tops of mountains and hills, and the custom carried over to the West, where his shrines often replaced the pagan cult shrines of the god Woden.

PATRON OF HOLY SOULS

In popular belief, Michael is charged to assist the dying, accompany their souls to their private judgment, bring them to purgatory, and afterward present them to God in Heaven.

"St. Martin [of Tours] Dividing His Cloak for the Beggar" by Anton Van Dyck (1599-1641) shows the saint as a 17th-century cavalier.

St. Michael the Archangel portrayed by a 15th-century Russian ikon.

Thus, he is the patron of the holy souls. This is the reason for dedicating cemetery chapels to him, and all over Europe thousands of such chapels bear his name. In past centuries, weekly Masses were offered in his honor and in favor of the departed ones in these chapels.

OTHER CUSTOMS

In northern Spain, Michael was acclaimed as the national patron of the Basques. Here his feast was kept with great celebration. His statue was brought from the national shrine to all churches of Navarre for a short visit annually so he could be honored and venerated by the faithful in their hometowns.

Some of the ancient lore of the Germanic nations has come down to our time in the form of St. Michael's parades, fairs, plays, and other customs.

In the north of Europe and in England, wine consumed on St. Michael's feast was called "St. Michael's Love" (*Michelsminne*).[1]

At the end of April 1893, there was a great drought in Sicily that lasted for six months. The Sicilian peasants appealed to their saints, as usual. All methods of procuring rain were tried without effect. Processions were held, candles were lit, and prayers were said. The peasants began to lose patience and banished many of their saints. At Palermo, they dumped their statue of St. Joseph in a garden to see the state of things for himself, and they swore to leave him there in the sun till rain fell. Other saints' statues were turned like naughty children with their faces to the wall. At Caltanisetta, the golden wings of St. Michael the Archangel were torn from his statue's shoulders and taken away. These were replaced with wings of pasteboard. The purple mantle on his statue was taken away and a rag wrapped about him instead.[2]

SCAPULAR

There is a scapular of St. Michael the Archangel worn by members of the archconfraternity of the same name. The confraternity was begun in the Church of St. Eustachius in Rome.

The two segments of cloth of this scapular are in the shape of a shield. One is blue and the other is black, as are the bands. Both sides of the scapular have the traditional representation of the Archangel St. Michael slaying the dragon, and carry the inscription *Quis ut Deus* ("Who is like God"). These words are attributed to St. Michael in the great battle at or near the beginning of time when he and his heavenly host fell upon the army of Lucifer and cast them forth from the Kingdom of Heaven into the abyss of hell.

CHAPLET OF ST. MICHAEL

The chaplet of St. Michael honors not only the great archangel but all of the heavenly spirits. This chaplet originated in 1751 when St. Michael appeared to a devout Portuguese Carmelite, Antonia d'Astonac. He requested her to publish in his honor a chaplet of nine salutations, each one of which corresponds to one of the nine choirs of angels. One Our Father and three Hail Marys are said in conjunction with each of the salutations. The chaplet concludes with four Our Fathers honoring Sts. Michael, Gabriel, Raphael, and the Guardian Angel. He promised to those who practiced the devotion faithfully that he would send an angel from each choir to accompany them when they received Holy Communion. He promised his assistance and that of all the Holy Angels during life to those who daily recited the chaplet, and to those faithful he also promised deliverance from the pains of Purgatory for themselves and the souls of their relatives. A group of Carmelite sisters who had experienced the spiritual benefits of this chaplet requested approval from Pope Pius IX, who indulgenced the chaplet in 1851.

The beads of this chaplet may be of a single color, usually black or white, or may be multicolored. One group of nuns made a nine-color chaplet based on the revelations of a German mystic. In the United States, the Oblates of St. Benedict distribute the chaplet, which also is made in nine colors. They have used the colors simply to separate the decades, and the colors do not have any special significance.

The chaplet is begun with an act of contrition and the recitation of the following invocation: "O God, come to my assistance. O Lord, make haste to help me. Glory be to the Father, etc."

The nine salutations are as follows:

1. By the intercession of St. Michael and the celestial Choir of Seraphim, may the Lord make us worthy to burn with the fire of perfect charity.

2. By the intercession of St. Michael and the celestial Choir of Cherubim, may the Lord vouchsafe to grant us grace to leave the ways of wickedness to run in the paths of Christian perfection.

3. By the intercession of St. Michael and the celestial Choir of Thrones, may the Lord infuse into our hearts a true and sincere spirit of humility.

4. By the intercession of St. Michael and the celestial Choir of Dominions, may the Lord give us grace to govern our senses and subdue our unruly passions.

5. By the intercession of St. Michael and the celestial Choir of Powers, may the Lord vouchsafe to protect our souls against the snares and temptations of the devil.

6. By the intercession of St. Michael and the celestial Choir of Virtues, may the Lord preserve us from evil and suffer us not to fall into temptation.

7. By the intercession of St. Michael and the celestial Choir of Principalities, may God fill our souls with a true spirit of obedience.

8. By the intercession of St. Michael and the celestial Choir of Archangels, may the Lord give us perseverance in faith and in all good works, in order that we may gain the glory of Paradise.

9. By the intercession of St. Michael and the celestial Choir of Angels, may the Lord grant us to be protected by them in this mortal life and conducted hereafter to eternal glory.

The chaplet is concluded with the following prayer: "O glorious Prince St. Michael, chief and commander of the heavenly hosts, guardian of souls, vanquisher of rebel spirits, servant in the house of the Divine King, and our admirable conductor, thou who dost shine with excellence and superhuman virtue, vouchsafe to deliver us from all evil, who turn to thee with confidence and enable us by thy gracious protection to serve God more and more faithfully every day. Pray for us, O glorious St. Michael, Prince of the Church of Jesus Christ, that we may be made worthy of His promises.

PRAYER FOR VICTORY IN BATTLE

St. Michael the Archangel, defend us in battle. Be our protection against the wickedness and snares of the devil. May God rebuke him, we humbly pray, and do thou, O prince of the heavenly host, by the power of God, thrust into hell Satan and all evil spirits who wander through the world for the ruin of souls.

OTHER ARCHANGELS

The other two of the seven archangels who are named in Scripture are Raphael and Gabriel.

In the Book of Tobit, Raphael was sent in human form as Azariah, the traveling companion of the young Tobiah (or Tobias) on his way to be the eighth husband of Sarah, whose seven previous husbands had been slain by a demon. Raphael bound the demon, Asmodeus, "in the desert of upper Egypt." Thus Sarah was delivered from the devil and her marriage to Tobiah was blessed. On this same journey, Raphael restored sight to Tobiah's father, who had been blind.

Raphael, or "Healer of God," is assumed to be the angel who, as told in John 5:4, "troubled the water" and "whosoever then first after the troubling of the water stepped in was made whole of whatsoever disease he had."

Raphael is invoked against all sickness — physical, mental or spiritual — and against possession by spirits. With Michael, he is known for his healing of the sick. He is the patron of doctors and nurses, lovers, travelers, and young and innocent people.

Gabriel is the angel of the annunciation to Mary (Luke 1:26) and the traditional trumpeter of the Last Judgment.

Blessed Michael, I praise you and I bless you for protecting our soldiers in the recent war in the mideast, and for assisting in its speedy conclusion. With Raphael, Gabriel, and all the angels, preserve me from harm, and accompany me on my journey through life.

Notes

1. Weiser, *The Holyday Book* (New York, 1956), p. 191.
2. Frazer, *The Golden Bough* (New York, 1940), p. 74-75.

St. Nicholas, Bishop, Patron of Children

St. Nicholas, the fourth-century Archbishop of Myra, is the patron of many places and people. He is the patron of Russia because of his reputation as protector of the weak and poor. He is patron of Venice because of a legend that he had shown power over the sea by quieting a storm while on a voyage to the Holy Land. Thieves looked to him for help because he once forced a gang of thieves to restore their plunder and brought them back to the right ways.

Young girls have a special place in the heart of this saint, as shown when he anonymously tossed three bags of gold into the window of three sisters who, for lack of dowry, could find no husbands and were about to be sold into prostitution. Even pawnbrokers are under his patronage. Some say the three gold balls which are the sign of a pawnshop are an adaptation of the three bags of gold provided by Nicholas for the three unhappy sisters.

There was a church dedicated to St. Nicholas at Constantinople from the sixth century. From the ninth century in the East and the eleventh in the West, he has been one of the most popular saints of Christendom. He is celebrated in pious custom and folklore, represented countless times in paintings and carvings; innumerable churches are named for him, and yet little factual information is known about him other than his being the bishop of Myra in Lycia (southwestern Asia Minor).

Legends, far-fetched and often childish, abound. One holds that he brought to life three children who had been murdered and hidden in a brine vat. Others say he miraculously saved three unjustly condemned men and rescued sailors in distress off the Lycian coast. Thus his patronage of children, criminals, and sailors.

Nicholas is reputed to have suffered for his faith before the ascent of Constantine, and he was supposedly present at the first general council at Nicea in 325. There is no historical support for either of these statements.

CUSTOMS

In the United States, St. Nicholas, patron of children, is the origin of Santa Claus. The name is derived from the Dutch dialect form of his name, Sinte Klaas.

In Europe, St. Nicholas does not come on Christmas Eve as he does here, but on the eve of his own feast, the night before December 6. There he does not come down the chimney but rings the doorbell. He is fat and jovial and carries a bag on his back containing cookies and fruits. St. Nick questions the youngsters about their behavior and their future intentions. If he is pleased, he gives them a treat with the promise of something more on Christmas, when the Christ child, not the saint, will bring the promised gifts.

Because Nicholas was quite young when he became a bishop, a custom arose in medieval England of celebrating St. Nicholas's Day by selecting a boy from the cathedral choir to be a mock-bishop for a term of office from December 6 to December 28. In full episcopal regalia and followed by a magnificent entourage, the boy-bishop put on a hilarious burlesque of the pomp and dignity of the real bishop. This custom was revived in several English cathedral towns in the middle of this century.[1]

RELICS

In 1034, when the shrine at Myra fell into the hands of the Saracens, several Italian cities vied for possession of the relics because of the saint's popularity and the phenomenon that attended his remains. The relics were removed in secret and enshrined at Bari in Apulia, where they still are. This is why he is sometimes called Nicholas of Bari. A new basilica was built to enshrine the relics with Pope Urban II presiding over its consecration.

A liquid exuded from the saint's bones, first observed at Myra and continuing at Bari. The liquid, according to examinations made by scientists from the University at Bari, is a combination of hydrogen and oxygen with an extremely low content of bacteria and is considered biologically pure. This liquid collects only on the bones of the saint and not on the walls or other surfaces of the tomb. Although there are five periods when the liquid was not observed for a few years at a time, the saints bones have given off this miraculous fluid continuously for centuries, and they still do today.[2]

Good St. Nicholas, bringer of gifts at Christmas time, give me the gift of keeping the spirit of Christmas in my heart all year through.

Notes
1. Harper, op. cit., p. 308.
2. Cruz, *Relics* (Huntington, Ind., 1984), p. 196.

St. Nicholas of Myra as portrayed by an 18th-century Russian ikon.

Top: St. Patrick. Below: Rock of Cashel, where he accidentally drove his staff into the foot of an Irish king, who thought it part of baptism.

St. Patrick, Bishop, Patron of Ireland

St. Patrick, the great evangelizer of the Irish, was born about the year 385. A Britannic Celt by race and a Roman citizen by nationality, he was the grandson of a priest and son of a civil official who was a Christian deacon. At sixteen, Patrick was captured by Gaels in a coastal raid and was taken from his father's land on the west coast of England to Ireland, where he spent six years in slavery as a herdsman. During this time, he developed an intense prayer life. At last he escaped on a ship to the continent and made his way home to a joyous family reunion in England.

At home, he was called in a dream to return to Ireland and preach Christ there. It is generally believed that he studied for the priesthood in Gaul, as a disciple of St. Germanus at Auxerre. About the year 432, he was ordained a priest and consecrated as bishop, after which he journeyed with some companions back to Ireland as a missionary.

Although there were already Christians in Ireland before the coming of St. Patrick, they had not made many converts. For almost thirty years, Patrick labored at the conversion of the island. He baptized thousands, organized the clergy, and established churches and religious communities. Toward the end of his life, he established the see of Armagh, which he held as archbishop and primate of Ireland until his death.

Patrick encountered much resistance from the Druidic priests and from some of the local kings; many vicious attempts were made to stop his work. In spite of threats, dangers, hardships, and calumnies, Patrick serenely continued with his work, fighting all obstacles with prayer, penance, and heroic patience. By the time of his death, the Church had set firm roots in the Irish nation, and his disciples completed his work, making all Ireland a blooming garden of Christianity.

Toward the end of his life, Patrick made a forty-day retreat on Cruachan Aigli in Mayo. This has been a site of pilgrimage for the Irish people ever since.

Soon after his death, accounts of the saint's life began to be embellished with fictional and legendary details. A number of these undoubtedly had a historical basis; others were simply the creations of the imaginative early Gaelic writers. Modern scholars have had a difficult task sorting historical facts from legendary and fictional details. The main contemporary evidence about Patrick's life is found in his own writing. He reviews his life and work in the autobiographical *Confession*, and one extant letter denounces an attack on one of his congregations by the British Chieftain Coroticus. The beautiful morning prayer the "Breastplate" (*Lorica*) is attributed to Patrick. In his writings, the reader can easily catch Patrick's sense of being called by God to the work he had undertaken and his sense of determination in carrying it out.

"I, Patrick, a sinner, am the most ignorant and of least account among the faithful, despised by many . . . I owe it to God's grace that so many people should through me be born again to Him."

St. Patrick was venerated greatly, beginning immediately after his death. There are many and varied legends concerning the saint. Some of the most famous ones are that he freed Ireland from all poisonous snakes and reptiles, that he received a miraculous staff from Christ in a vision and thereafter always carried it with him, that he lived to be a hundred twenty years old, and that he was given the privilege of judging the Irish race at the end of time.

In art, Patrick is shown as a bishop, and his emblems are snakes and the shamrock.

St. Patrick is popular and venerated among other races and nations beside the Irish. He is invoked as a local patron in several parts of Europe. In one region of Austria, for example, he is a favored patron of farmers and their domestic animals.

The celebration of St. Patrick's feast day on March 17 consists of some traditional details which are faithfully kept in

Ireland and which have spread across the ocean to the United States. The day begins with attendance at Mass in the morning. Then follows a solemn parade with a subsequent meeting and speeches, festive meals in the homes, and entertainment for the evening. The city of New York hosts one of the largest of the traditional St. Patrick's day parades; on March 17 people of all ethnic origins seem to turn Irish.

The custom of wearing green did not begin until over a thousand years after Patrick's death. The custom of wearing the shamrock, however, is based on a legend that St. Patrick used the trefoil that he found growing near Cashel to teach King Oengus the doctrine of the Holy Trinity. Just as the shamrock has three leaves on one stem, so too there are three persons in one God.

In Ireland, the men displayed the shamrock on their hats. Ladies wore a cross made of ribbons on their dress. A special drink called "St. Patrick's poteen" was drunk. In the United States, people often drink green-dyed beer at their celebrations.

The saint's feast marked the beginning of spring in Ireland, and it is still regarded as the best time for the farmers to begin planting their potatoes. The livestock are driven out to pasture on that day.

Many modern scholars place the date of Patrick's death as March 17, 461, although it may have been as late as 493. In the church cemetery next to the great Cathedral of Down, there is an enormous granite slab engraved with the name Padraig in Celtic letters. It is believed that this stone marks the place of the saint's burial. A handbell once belonging to the saint is kept as a treasured relic in the National Museum of Dublin.

LORICA (BREASTPLATE OF ST. PATRICK)

The Book of Armagh ascribes the authorship of the beautiful prayer called "Breastplate" or *Lorica* to St. Patrick, and it may be that he composed it. Millions of faithful have used it through the centuries with devotion. Here are some verses from this famous prayer in a traditional English version.

> I arise today
> Through God's strength to pilot me,
> God's might to uphold me,
> God's wisdom to guide me,
> God's eye to look before me,
> God's ear to hear me,
> God's word to speak for me,
> God's hand to guard me,
> God's way to lie before me,
> God's shield to protect me,
> God's host to save me
> From snares of devils,
> From temptations of vices,
> From everyone who shall wish me ill,
> Afar and near,
> Alone and in a multitude.
> — *St. Patrick*

Beloved St. Patrick, teach me as you taught the Irish kings the love of the Holy Trinity. Chase the venomous snakes of sin from my heart. Above all, help me to imitate your humility and your passion for leading others to Christ.

St. Paul, Apostle and Missionary, Patron of Preachers and Tentmakers

A Jew of the tribe of Benjamin, pupil of the great rabbi Gamaliel, Saul was a Pharisee, a learned rabbi, and a scrupulous observer of the Mosaic Law. The man who became Paul was a Roman citizen, born at Tarsus in Cilicia. Highly educated, he spoke both Aramaic and Greek. Physically, Paul is believed to have been a man of short stature, somewhat bald, with broad shoulders, a fair complexion, and a thick grayish beard.

The new Christian faith was an abomination to Paul, and he personally took on the responsibility of exterminating it. Furious, he went to the High Priest and got an order to go to Damascus, arrest every Christian he could find, and bring them all in chains to Jerusalem.

On the last day of the journey, Saul and his companions were suddenly surrounded by a brilliant light. Falling to the ground, Saul heard the voice of Jesus. In one of the most dramatic and important events in Christian history, Saul of Tarsus, blasphemer and persecutor of Christians, became Paul the Apostle, one of God's main instruments in the conversion of the world.

"Lord, what wilt Thou have me do ?" Saul asked. His great missionary journeys from then on took him to every part of the known world. He was finally beheaded at Rome toward the end of the reign of Nero, probably around the year 67.

Saul changed his name to Paul in honor of Sergius Paulus, whom he converted to Christianity.

The fourteen letters left by St. Paul and his followers powerfully express the Church's doctrine and have been the consolation and delight of many throughout the ages.

HIS PATRONAGE

Paul is the patron of preachers and theologians, ropemakers, weavers, and tentmakers. Throughout his career, he financed his ministry by practicing the tentmaker's trade. Paul's aid is invoked against snakebite, against hail, for acceptance of the circumstances of daily living, and for a holy death.

CUSTOMS

An old English folksong chimes, "If St. Paul's Day be fair and clear, it does betide a happy year." St. Paul's Day (January 25) gives advance information about the weather and more. The rest of the song refers to the conditions of rain, clouds, and wind, claiming that it is possible to foretell what will be the price of grain, the health of livestock, and the prospects of war. The song was already old when it was translated from Latin to English, and most of western Europe had believed it for many centuries.[1]

In Hungary, grain was blessed after Mass on Peter and Paul's Day (June 29). People wove crowns, crosses and other religious symbols from straw, had them blessed, and carried them on wooden poles in procession around the church. Afterwards these were taken home and kept suspended from the ceiling over the dining table. There is also a special blessing of bread in Hungary on this day.[2]

HIS RELICS

The place of Paul's execution is believed to be the site where the Church of San Paolo Alle Tre Fontane is now located. This church is also called the Church of the Decapitation, and it was built in the fifth century on the spot where tradition related that Paul was beheaded. In the sanctuary today, two major relics are kept of the apostle — a low marble column to which he was bound and a marble slab on which he died. At the back of the church are three small buildings protecting three fountains which are said to have miraculously bubbled forth when the saint's head made three bounces on the slope.

The actual head of the saint is enshrined together with that of St. Peter in a golden urn enclosed in the papal altar of the Lateran.

Under Roman law, the bodies of the executed could be given to family or friends for burial, and it is believed the body of St. Paul was buried on property belonging to a Roman noblewoman named Lucina. A simple mortuary chapel was constructed over the grave until Constantine replaced it with a basilica that was consecrated by Pope Sylvester I on the same day that St. Peter's Basilica was consecrated in 324. The basilica was enlarged and endowed by many nobles including Constantine, St. Gregory the Great, and Charlemagne. Today this church is known as the Basilica of St. Paul's Outside the Walls. The saint's body is kept beneath a marble slab dating from the fourth century.[3]

PRAYER FOR A HOLY DEATH

O Glorious St. Paul, on earth thou wast a mirror of innocence and a model of penance. Thy life was spent in bringing back the erring souls of countless unfortunate sinners. Do mercifully look down once more from Heaven and hear my petition. Obtain for me so great a love of Jesus that I may make His sufferings mine. Let me realize in the wounds of my Savior the wickedness of my transgressions, and obtain from them, as from the fountain of salvation, the grace of bitter tears and a resolution to imitate thee in thy penance. Finally, intercede for me that I may, by the grace of God, die a holy death and come at last to enjoy with thee His blessed presence in Heaven for all eternity.[4]

PRAYER FOR ACCEPTANCE

O glorious St. Paul, who didst suffer prison, beatings, criticism, stonings, and all manner of persecutions, obtain for us the grace to accept the infirmities, sufferings, and misfortunes of this life with grace and with fortitude, secure in the knowledge that no burden beyond our strength will be placed upon us. Pray for us, St. Paul the Apostle.[5]

PRINCES OF THE APOSTLES

St. Paul and St. Peter have been traditionally accorded the title of Princes of the Apostles. Both died as a result of the persecutions of Nero, Peter by crucifixion in the public circus or amphitheater at the Vatican hill and Paul outside the city. Special celebrations were held in their honor by Christians from earliest times.

Holy Apostle Paul, inflame me with your love for our Lord. Help me to witness to my faith by using all the graces God has given me.

Notes

1. Harper, *Days and Customs of All Faiths* (New York, 1957), p. 32.

2. Weiser, *Handbook of Christian Feasts and Customs* (New York, 1958), p. 333.

3. Cruz, *Relics* (Huntington, Ind., 1984), p. 124.

4. Anna Riva, *Devotions to the Saints* (Toluca Lake, Calif., 1982), p. 62.

5. Ibid., p. 63.

Heroic St. Paul (flanked by a similar statue of St. Peter) guards the steps and the entrance to the Vatican Basilica in St. Peter's Square.

Crucifixion of St. Peter is shown in medieval dress in this detail from a painting by an unknown French artist of the early 15th century.

St. Peter, Apostle, Pontiff, Martyr, Patron of Fishermen and Locksmiths

Simon Peter, an uneducated, rough-and-ready fisherman, is always first in any list of apostles. Simon and his brother Andrew, along with the sons of Zebedee, James and John, were partners in a fishing venture on the Sea of Galilee. Peter was fishing when he was called to follow Christ and be a "fisher of men."

Originally from Bethsaida, Simon, his wife, and her family were living in Capernaum when he was called by the Lord. Simon declared, "Thou art the Christ, the Son of the Living God." In reply, Jesus said, "Thou art Peter, and upon this rock I will build my church." (Peter was called Cephas, or Kepha in Aramaic, which is the equivalent of the Greek word *Petros*, or rock.) Jesus conferred on him the "keys of the kingdom of Heaven" and the powers of "binding and loosing."

Peter was present at all major events of Jesus' public ministry and, along with James and John, witnessed the raising of Jairus's daughter, the Transfiguration, and the Agony in the Garden. Impetuous, hasty, and outspoken, Peter was the leader of the apostles. After the Resurrection, Peter was the first of the apostles to whom Jesus appeared, and subsequently the risen Lord reiterated Peter's responsibilities: "Feed my lambs. . . . Feed my sheep" (John 21:15-19). In spite of his denial of Christ before the crucifixion, afterwards Peter fearlessly preached to the crowds after Pentecost, and he performed many miracles in the name of Christ. .

Tradition claims Peter was crucified head downward during the persecutions of the emperor Nero in Rome, about A.D. 64-67. This tradition has been questioned from time to time, but research of modern scholars has done much to confirm the tradition, although the manner of crucifixion is uncertain. St. Peter's Basilica has always been believed to be situated over his tomb. Catholics acclaim Peter as the first Pope, and out of respect for his primacy, no other Pope has ever taken his name.

HIS EMBLEM IN ART

St. Peter's emblem in art is two crossed keys, symbolizing the keys of the kingdom of Heaven promised by Jesus (Matthew 16:19).

HIS RELICS

In addition to the bones of the saint kept in the Vatican, there is also a chair believed to have been used by Peter in the house of Pudens, where he lodged on first coming to Rome. Its solid legs of yellow oak have iron rings attached to them through which rods were placed enabling it to function as a portable throne for the early popes. The chair was on exhibit for centuries, but in 1656 Bernini was commissioned to design a monument for it. His massive sculpture was dedicated in 1666, with long and elaborate ceremonies and the chair was fitted into its place behind Bernini's black, gilt, and bronze throne. Until the beginning of the last century, it could be seen by visitors who climbed a ladder to the rear. At the last examination of the relic in 1867, it was revealed that the chair had been ruthlessly gouged by relic hunters. The Feast of the Chair of St. Peter was celebrated from the early days of the Christian era to honor the preeminent position Christ gave to Peter as leader of His Church, of which the chair is a symbol.

During the saint's stay with Pudens, he used a wooden table for the celebration of Holy Mass which was regarded by the host as a treasured relic. It was taken to the catacombs and carefully preserved there through the years of persecution. It was used as an altar in hiding by the early popes. Later it was entrusted to the Church of St. Pudentiana, and still later transferred to the Lateran, the cathedral church of Rome. A portion of the table was retained at St. Pudentiana's and is kept in a chapel dedicated to St. Peter. For years the altar was left exposed in the Lateran, but it is now encased in an altar of marble with the original wood still visible. It is the principal altar of the Lateran and is known as the papal altar.

Atop this altar is a magnificent Gothic structure resting on four marble columns. In the upper part of this canopy, in a chamber behind a bronze lattice, are preserved the heads of St. Peter and St. Paul.

The chains of St. Peter from his imprisonment in Jerusalem and those from his imprisonment in the Mamertine Prison are the subject of a reported miracle during the time of Pope Leo the Great. When the pope compared the two chains, they miraculously fused together into one series of links. Because of this miracle, the Empress Eudocia built the Basilica of St. Peter in Chains and dedicated it to the apostle in the year 442. The relic is kept in a golden urn beneath the high altar.

A leather sandal believed to have been worn by the saint is preserved in the Cathedral of Oviedo, Spain. The sandal has been described by experts as a Roman sandal dating from the first or second century. It is enclosed in a silver case from the seventeenth century, and documents indicate it may have been a present from a pope to a king of Spain in the ninth or tenth century.[1]

CUSTOMS

Possibly stemming from the ancient Germanic mythology of the gods Thor and Woden, after their conversion the Christianized Germanic people seem to have invested St. Peter and St. Paul with the function of "weather makers." Many legends ascribe thunder and lightning to some activity of Peter in Heaven such as bowling. When it snows, St. Peter is "shaking out his feather bed."[2]

In several villages of Navarre, France, prayers for rain used to be offered to St. Peter. By way of enforcing these, the villagers carried the image of the saint in procession to the river, where they thrice invited him to reconsider his resolution and to grant their prayers; then, if he was still obstinate, they plunged him in the water in spite of remonstrances of the clergy, who pleaded that a simple caution or admonition administered to the image would produce an equally good effect. After this the rain was sure to fall within twenty-four hours.[3]

In the rural sections of the Alpine countries when the church bells ring the Angelus early in the morning of June 29, people step under the trees in their gardens and kneel down to pray. After the prayer, they bow and make the sign of the cross, believing that on St. Peter's Day the blessing of the Holy Father in Rome is carried by angels throughout the world to all who sincerely await it.[4]

The faithful traditionally visit the tomb of St. Peter in the Vatican Basilica. Here there is a bronze statue of the saint and pilgrims devoutly kiss the foot of the statue and pray for the intentions of the Holy Father.

ST. PETER'S PLANT

Various flowers and herbs are under St. Peter's patronage, especially those with a hairy stem. The Peter's Plant (*primula hirsuta*) is collected, dried, and kept to be used as a medicinal tea, especially useful against bites of snakes and dogs.

HIS PATRONAGE

Along with Paul, Peter is often invoked against snakebites, and custom has it that one who prays especially well on St. Peter and St. Paul's feast day will not be bitten by a snake during the coming year. Peter is patron of fishermen and sailors, of leather merchants, locksmiths, shoemakers, cobblers, and watchmakers. He is often invoked against fever because Christ cured his mother-in-law of fever. He is prayed to particularly for strength and for forgiveness of sins. From the tenth century on, he was venerated as the heavenly gatekeeper who guards the gates of eternity and admits or turns away souls.

PRAYER FOR FORGIVENESS OF SINS

Blessed Apostle Peter, to whom God has given the keys of the kingdom of Heaven and the power to bind and loose, grant that we may be delivered through the help of your intercession from the bonds of our sins.

O Holy Shepherd, Prince of the Apostles, pray for us that we may be made worthy of the promises of Christ.

Notes
1. Cruz, *Relics* (Huntington, Ind., 1984), p. 129.
2. Weiser, *Handbook of Christian Feasts and Customs* (New York, 1958) p. 333.
3. Frazer, op. cit., 1940, p. 77.
4. Weiser, op. cit., p. 334.

St. Rita of Cascia, Widow, Nun, Patron for Impossible Causes

St. Rita was born at Spoleto, Italy, in 1381. As a young girl, she dreamed of entering a convent and begged her parents for permission. They denied her wish and arranged a marriage for her. Thus, at the tender age of twelve, Marguerita was married to Paolo Ferdinando.

Rita became a good wife and mother in spite of the fact that her husband was a man of violent temper who often mistreated his wife. He taught their children his own evil ways. In spite of this, Rita tried to perform her duties faithfully and to pray and receive the sacraments frequently. After nearly twenty years of marriage, Rita's husband was murdered. In his last years, he had repented because of Rita's constant prayers for him.

Shortly after the death of her husband, both of her sons died, leaving Rita alone in the world. She filled her days with prayer, fasting, penances of many kinds, and charitable works.

At last she was admitted to the convent of the Augustinian nuns at Cascia in Umbria, where she lived a life of perfect obedience and great charity. At first Rita was denied entrance, but she was accepted after the bolted doors and gates of the monastery were miraculously opened for her by her patron saints.

Rita was especially devoted to the passion of Christ. After being inspired by a sermon preached by St. James of the Marches, Rita prayed to participate in some way with Our Lord in His suffering. In a mystical experience, one of the thorns from the crucifix struck her on the forehead, leaving a deep wound which did not heal. This festered and produced such an offensive odor that for the next 15 years she stayed in virtual seclusion.

A number of other supernatural happenings are reported in her life, although these cannot be well substantiated because the only extant biography of her was written a hundred fifty years after her death.

Three days before her death, Rita was favored with a vision of Our Lord and His Mother. She died on May 22, 1457. At her death, her cell was filled with an extraordinary perfume, and a light emanated from the wound on her forehead. The bells of the city began ringing of their own volition.

The body was placed in the church, and the miracles reported by the many pilgrims to her bier were so numerous, and the perfume that filled the church was so intense, that the civil and ecclesiastical authorities allowed the body to be placed in a position between the cloister and the church where the body could be venerated by both pilgrims and cloistered nuns. The body remained in this position for over one hundred fifty years without a proper entombment. When the remains were examined prior to her beatification, the body was discovered to be in a good state of preservation. A report from this time, 1627, states that the eyes of the relic opened unaided and remained open for some time as paintings done during that time indicate. The body seemed to move to one side and after a lapse of some years returned to its original position. One recorded observation said that the body was elevated to the top of the sarcophagus.

RELICS AND CUSTOMS

Rita was canonized in 1900, and her devotion spread rapidly beyond Italy to Europe and the Americas. A new basilica was built in her honor at Cascia in 1946. Here, the saint's miraculously preserved body is housed in a golden shrine.

A heavenly sweet smell is frequently noticed at the shrine. Although it is not continuous, the odor is sometimes observed at the time of some miracles.

An interesting relic is growing in the courtyard of the

convent. In order to test her obedience, her superior handed Rita a piece of dry wood and ordered her to plant it and water it daily. The stick sprouted into a healthy grapevine that still bears fruit. Every year the harvest of grapes is divided among high-ranking ecclesiastics. The leaves are dried, made into a powder, and sent to the sick around the world.

THE BEES OF ST. RITA

When she was an infant, according to biographies, tiny white bees were once seen swarming around Rita's mouth. About two hundred years after her death in 1457, a unique variety of bees began living in a fifteenth-century wall of the monastery and have lived there continuously ever since. These bees remain in hibernation for ten months of the year and emerge during Holy Week. The bees are never seen to leave the convent enclosure, and after a few weeks of activity about the gardens of the convent, they return to the wall after the Feast of St. Rita and seal themselves into holes they have made themselves. The sisters of the convent of Cascia do not consider their presence to be anything other than a natural occurrence which by an unusual coincidence occurs in the walls of their convent.[1]

THE SANTA RITA #1

One of the most famous oil wells in Texas is the Santa Rita Number One. This well, drilled on state-owned lands, opened the field that pumped riches into the University of Texas, where the original pump is displayed today in Austin. The name originated with a group of Catholic women from New York who had invested in stock sold by the driller. They asked that the well be named for St. Rita, as patron of the impossible. After the driller completed the derrick over the well, he

St. Rita of Cascia, a wonder-worker like St. Jude, is shown receiving the stigma of a thorn in her forehead on a typical Italian holy card.

St. Thérèse of Lisieux as she looked in her last photo, taken in the convent garden three months before her death in September 1897.

climbed to the top, sprinkled dried rose petals which had been blessed in the saint's name and given him by the investors, and christened the well.[2]

PRAYER TO ST. RITA

O glorious St. Rita, thou who didst share in a marvelous manner the sorrowful passion of our Lord Jesus Christ, get me the grace to suffer in patience the miseries of this life and be my refuge in all my necessities.

— The Raccolta

Dear St. Rita, friend to all who hope for the impossible, I beg your intercession for all my hopes and dreams for this life. More importantly, however, I beg you assist me in obtaining all the graces needed to live this life in order to be happy in Heaven in the next.

Notes

1. Cruz, op. cit., pp. 283-284.
2. Ann Ball, *A Handbook of Catholic Sacramentals* (Huntington, Ind., 1991), p. 197.

St. Thérèse of Lisieux, Virgin, Patroness of Foreign Missions

A young French Carmelite nun, Sister Thérèse of the Child Jesus and the Holy Face, lay in agony. Tuberculosis had attacked not only her lungs but her entire body. Death was imminent. She indicated that with her death, her true mission would begin, ". . . my mission of making God loved as I love Him, to give my little way to souls. If God answers my request . . . I want to spend my Heaven in doing good upon earth."

At the time of her death in 1897, no one would have suspected that scarcely twenty-seven years later the life and heroic virtues of this quiet, retiring young Carmelite would be held up to the world as an example of the Gospel ideal of sanctity as a daily following of Christ without heroics or display. In the Bull of Canonization, Pius XI expressed this beautifully when he stated that "Without going beyond the common order of things in her way of life, she followed out and fulfilled her vocation with such alacrity, generosity, and constancy that she reached a heroic degree of virtue."

In her writing, Thérèse had developed a doctrine of abandonment and love. God did not require great deeds, only love. She discovered that love is to admit the need of love, and to express that need in prayer to Love Himself, Christ. She teaches us that God puts within us the desire for Himself and only He can satisfy that desire. To accept any other source for human happiness leads only to despair.*

Thérèse Martin was born at Alençon in January of 1873, the last of nine children born to Louis and Zelie Martin. At fourteen, Thérèse determined to enter the Carmelites. After obtaining the necessary dispensation, she entered at the age of fifteen.

For the next nine years, Thérèse lived the doctrine and theory of sanctity without in any way going out of the ordinary. In the cloister, she followed the rule exactingly, obeyed her superiors, suffered from aridity of spirit, laughed, attempted to get along with the differing personalities of her twenty-six sisters in religion, prayed, and, most of all, practiced her little way of self-denial and renunciation. Externally, she appeared simply as a good Carmelite should.

On Thérèse's death, copies of her autobiography, *Story of a Soul,* were circulated among the Carmelites and a few friends. Her doctrine of "the little way" was so startling, however, that more and more demand for its teaching arose. In 1906 a cause for her Beatification was entered in Rome, and by 1912 the fame of her sanctity had spread to the United States. Pius XI canonized Thérèse in 1925. Had she lived, she would only have been fifty-two years old in the year of her canonization.

All four of Thérèse's sisters lived to see her raised to the honors of the altar. They rejoiced with the countless others, well over sixty thousand at the canonization ceremony alone, who saw in Thérèse the embodiment of a spirituality open to all Christians in any state of life.

HER EMBLEM IN ART

St. Thérèse is generally pictured in the Carmelite habit, holding a crucifix and a bouquet of roses. She is quoted as having said that after death she would let forth a shower of roses (graces) on earth.

HER PATRONAGES

Although she never left her cloister, St. Thérèse has been named patroness of foreign missions, fulfilling a great childhood desire to be a missionary. Non-flying patroness of aviators, Thérèse is also invoked for the forgiveness of drunkenness, for the love of all persons, and to restore faith.

THE CHAPLET OF ST. THÉRÈSE

One of the greatest apostles of St. Thérèse in the New World was Father Albert Dolan. Gifted both as a preacher and as a writer, he introduced St. Thérèse and her "little way of spiritual childhood" to millions. He founded the Society of the Little Flower in 1923.

The chaplet of St. Thérèse stems from and is promoted by the society. The chaplet is a private devotion which both honors the saint and invokes her intercession. There are twenty-four beads in honor of the twenty-four years of her life. One additional bead and a medal of the saint complete the chaplet. On the single bead, an invocation to St. Thérèse as Patroness of the Missions is said: "St. Thérèse of the Child Jesus, Patroness of Missions, pray for us." A Glory Be is recited on each of the other beads in thanksgiving to the Holy Trinity for having given us the young saint and her "little way." It is customary to recite the chaplet in novena (nine days) or for a period of twenty-four days.

ST. THÉRÈSE'S PERSONAL PRAYER

Govern by all Thy wisdom, O Lord, so that my soul may always be serving Thee as Thou dost will and not as I may choose. Do not punish me, I beseech Thee, by granting that which I wish or ask if it offend Thy love, which would always live in me. Let me die to myself, so that I may serve Thee; let me live to Thee, who in Thyself art the true life.

Dear St. Thérèse, guide me in your little way that I may ascend to the heights of Heaven.

Note
* Boniface Hanley, O.F.M., *That Martin Girl* (Paterson, N.J., 1979), p. 29.

St. Valentine, Martyr, Patron of Greetings

The legend of St. Valentine tells of a young priest who lived in Rome in the third century. He was jailed for refusing to renounce his Christian faith. In prison, Valentine supposedly sent notes to his loved ones using a dove that came and sat in his cell window. The messages simply said, "Remember your Valentine."

Valentine, along with St. Marius and his family, assisted the martyrs who suffered during the reign of Claudius II. After his arrest, according to his "acts," the Prefect of Rome first imprisoned him, then had him beaten with clubs and beheaded. While in prison, he restored sight to the little blind daughter of his judge, Asterius, who thereupon was converted with all his family and suffered martyrdom with the saint. The date of his martyrdom is thought to be about 270.

A medieval version of the legend says that shortly before his execution, Valentine had sent a note to the kind daughter of his prison master. This legend was obviously intended to provide a belated reason for the already existing custom of the day.

There was a Church of St. Valentine built on the Flaminian Way in Rome in the middle of the fourth century. It is possible that Valentine was of Persian descent. Records of a martyred bishop at Terni may simply refer to the priest-martyr Valentine.

CUSTOMS

The custom of choosing a partner and sending "valentines" on February 14 apparently arose from the old idea that birds begin to pair on that day. There is no doubt, however, that the historical origin of the Valentine lore is based on a coincidence of dates. The pagan Romans celebrated Lupercalia, a great feast, on February 15. The feast was in honor of the pastoral god Lupercus, who is an equivalent of the Greek god Pan. On the eve of the feast, as a part of it, the young people held a celebration of their own, declaring their love for each other, proposing marriage, or choosing sweethearts for the following year. In some places, the boys drew names to choose their partners. These names were worn pinned to the sleeves of the young men. (Even today, we say a man wears his heart on his sleeve when he shows his interest in a young lady.) The couples sometimes exchanged presents. The Roman youth festival was under the patronage of the goddess Juno Februata. After the Roman Empire became Christian, the feast was changed to the patronage of the saint whose feast was celebrated on February 14, the priest and martyr Valentine.

Proof of the Roman origin of the Valentine lore is the fact that in countries of Roman historical background even small details like the games of chance and other customs were continued into the late Middle Ages, while in other countries these details are missing and St. Valentine as patron of young lovers is the only observance.[1]

In Germany, Austria, and among the western Slavs, Laetare Sunday used to be the day to announce the engagements of young people. In Bohemia, the boys would send messengers to the homes of their girl friends to deliver the proposal. In Austria, the girls of each village lined up in front of the church after Mass, and their boy friends would take them by the hand and lead them back into the house of God, thus "proposing" to them by a silent act of religious import. After the couple prayed together, they would seal the engagement with a special meal. These engagement customs were called "Valentine," although they did not take place on St. Valentine's Day. The name is explained by the fact that St. Valentine was already considered the heavenly patron of young lovers and engaged couples.[2]

In southern Europe of the seventeenth century, a hopeful maiden ate a hard-boiled egg and pinned five bay leaves to her pillow before going to sleep on Valentine's Eve, believing this would make her dream of her future husband.

CARDS

Our American custom of sending Valentine cards is unknown in the countries of northern Europe. This custom came from England. The traditional words actually imply: "You are my Valentine, and I offer you my companionship, affection, and love for the next twelve months and am willing to consider marriage if this companionship proves satisfactory for both of us."[3]

The Duke of Orléans is believed to have made the first Valentine card while imprisoned in the Tower of London in 1415. He wrote love poems to his wife in France. Sweethearts exchanged handmade cards in some places during the seventeenth and eighteenth centuries. In France, these were huge paper hearts trimmed with yards of real lace.

In the United States, Valentine cards became popular during the Civil War. Elaborate cards trimmed with spun glass, satin ribbons and sometimes mother-of-pearl ornaments were sold. For a time, Valentine's Day was as big an event as Christmas.[4]

HIS RELICS

On November 10, 1836, Valentine's relics were placed in the Carmelite church on Whitefriars Street in Dublin, Ireland. A humble Carmelite priest, Father John Spratt, had been tireless in his efforts for the stricken poor of the Dublin Liberties. On a brief visit to Rome, he was surprised by a gift from Pope Gregory XVI, given as a mark of the pontiff's esteem for the hardworking priest. The gift was the remains of St. Valentine, who also, in life, had a wide reputation for

St. Valentine's statue and the casket containing his relics, kept by the Carmelite Fathers at the Whitefriar Street Church in Dublin, Ireland.

St. Barbara was painted standing on top of cannon by Artilleryman Donald Beaman in the artillery headquarters at Fort Riley, Kansas.

holiness and self-denial. The relics were removed from the cemetery of St. Hippolytus in Rome and dispatched on the long journey to Dublin. Here they were enshrined in the church on Whitefriars Street for the glory of God and the veneration of the faithful.

Today St. Valentine's feast is still celebrated on February 14. The crocus, which blooms around this time of the year, is St. Valentine's flower. To this day St. Valentine is honored as a patron for lovers and sweethearts. For Catholics, he remains a symbol not only of our love for one another but also the love between God and man.

St. Valentine, help us to remain constant in our love of God in spite of all human trials. Assist us to show our love of God by spreading His love to all our brothers and sisters in Christ. Amen.

Notes

1. F.X. Weiser, *Handbook of Christian Feasts and Customs* (New York, 1958), p. 319.

2. Weiser, ibid., p. 185.

3. Weiser, ibid., p. 319.

4. Natalie Fantony, in *New Book of Knowledge* (New York, 1968), p. 266.

Sing a Song of All Saints

A saint is a person who has attained to the presence of God in Heaven. The calendar is full of saints days, honoring those departed souls who have been officially judged to have reached this blissful state. One small volume cannot even list all those known. Here then are some brief notes in our song, our litany to the saints.

APOLLONIA, DEACONESS, MARTYR

The next time you have a toothache, say a prayer to St. Apollonia, patroness of those with teeth problems.

Nothing reliable is known of Apollonia's early life in Egypt, but one legend holds that when she was only a small child an angel took her from her family and presented her to one of St. Anthony's disciples, who promptly baptized her and took her to Alexandria, dressed in white, to preach. Her father went to the authorities, and presumably she was returned home for quite some time.

Many years later, in 249 during a riot against Christians, the Alexandrian mob put several of them to death, including this aged deaconess. Repeatedly she was struck in the face, her teeth broken; then a bonfire was made and her tormentors threatened to burn her alive if she did not renounce her faith. After uttering a short prayer, she walked into the flames and was consumed. The particulars of her execution were related in a letter by St. Dionysius, who was bishop of Alexandria at the time. Her symbols in art are pincers and a tooth, and she is sometimes pictured with a golden tooth on a chain around her neck.

BARBARA, VIRGIN, MARTYR

The legend of St. Barbara tells that her father, a wealthy pagan, kept her shut up in a tower so she would not fall in love and leave him. In art, she is often shown imprisoned in a fort-like structure or with a tower.

Barbara was converted and secretly baptized by a priest named Valentinian, the story goes. Her father, on discovering her religion, took her before a judge. She was tortured and sentenced to be beheaded. Her father offered to carry out the sentence himself and was killed by lightning.

Barbara and Juliana, another Christian woman who had been martyred, were buried together. Soon there were reports of many healings at their graves.

Barbara lived and died at Nicomedia about the third century. She is named as the protector of artillerymen and miners and is invoked against storms, fire, lightning, explosions, and other forms of death so sudden that victims have no time to receive the Sacraments. All these functions have been assigned to Barbara because of stories and legends about her which are not accepted as historically true. No mention is made of the saint in any of the authoritative writings of her time, but by the seventh century she was firmly established in the hearts of many Christians.

Barbara's most important patronage is that against sudden death, and in medieval times she was universally invoked with prayers and hymns to grant a peaceful and well-prepared death. In many sections of Europe her feast day was a holy day. Miners, in particular, chose her as a special patroness because they were constantly exposed to danger of sudden death in their work.

In some parts of Europe the custom of "St. Barbara's Branch" was still practiced to the middle of this century. On December 4, small branches were broken from fruit trees and put in a pitcher of water in the kitchen or other warm room of the house. The branches broke into bloom around Christmas. If there were many blossoms, it was an indication of good luck. If the twig bloomed on Christmas it indicated that no one in the family would die in the coming year. Leaving aside such superstitious ideas, the Barbara Branch had a religious dimension, as it was used to decorate the manger scene.

BARTHOLOMEW, APOSTLE, MARTYR

Bartholomew's name is found in the lists of the apostles, but nowhere else in the New Testament. Because Bartholomew, meaning "Son of Talmai," is a surname, not a personal name, some scholars think that he may be the person mentioned as Nathanael or Nathaniel, whom the Lord praised for his innocence and simplicity of heart. If so, he was a devout resident of Cana who, upon hearing Jesus came from the rival town of Nazareth, asked, "Can anything good come from Nazareth?" After meeting Jesus, Bartholomew became among the first to declare Christ "the Son of God, the King of Israel."

Legend says he preached in Egypt, Persia, Mesopotamia, India, and was martyred in Armenia by being skinned alive and beheaded.

In accordance with his legend, St. Bartholomew is represented in art holding the knife which was used to flay him alive and dominating the figure of a vanquished devil. In Portugal, he is invoked against demonic possession, in epilepsy and in "fear" difficulties such as stammering, or in children's difficulties in walking or talking.

Bookbinders, butchers, and plasterers count him their patron.

BERNARD OF CLAIRVAUX, ABBOT, DOCTOR

St. Bernard of Clairvaux is counted as a co-founder of the Cistercian Order that emerged from the abbey of Citeaux. One of six brilliant sons of a Bergundian nobleman, Bernard decided to join the new monastery at Citeaux in 1113. He convinced four of his brothers and twenty-seven of his friends to come with him. Within two years, he was sent to establish a new house at Clairvaux. This monastery prospered and grew, sprouting nearly seventy other monasteries in France, England, and Ireland.

Bernard's personal fame spread quickly, in spite of his diffident nature, and he was drawn into public affairs. He attacked luxury among the clergy and persecution of Jews, preached against the Albigensian heresy, and stirred up enthusiasm for the Second Crusade. In spite of his immense activity and chronic ill health, this abbot and theologian was a prolific writer. Two of his most famous writings are the treatise "On the Love of God" and his sermons to his monks, "On the Song of Songs." Pope Pius VIII named him a Doctor of the Church in 1830. His emblem in art is a beehive.

One of the most beautiful of the Marian prayers, the Memorare, is attributed to St. Bernard.

THE MEMORARE OF ST. BERNARD

Remember, O most gracious Virgin Mary, that never was it known that anyone who fled to thy protection, implored thy help, or sought thy intercession was left unaided. Inspired with this confidence, I fly unto thee, O Virgin of virgins, my Mother. To thee I come; before thee I stand, sinful and sorrowful. O Mother of the Word Incarnate, despise not my petitions, but, in thy mercy, hear and answer me. Amen.

BERNARD OF MONTJOUX, HOSPITALER

The name of St. Bernard of Montjoux is remembered today mainly because of the Alpine passes and the big dogs that bear his name. These immense, kind-faced animals went out with little kegs of brandy fastened to their collars and rescued travelers lost in the Alpine snows.

Two mountain hospices were founded by Bernard at two particularly hazardous passes, more than seven thousand feet above sea level and choked with snow year round. Today these passes are known as the Great and the Little St. Bernard. The saint was disturbed by the ignorance and paganism of the people who lived in the rough mountain villages, and although there is little certainty about his early life, he apparently gave up wealth and high position to devote his life to the instruction and conversion of these people. Soon he realized that these two passes were death traps for travelers, and he built the two hospices about the year 962, collecting endowments for them and staffing them with Augustinian monks. (The dogs came much later.) Today as in previous centuries, monks from these two houses of mercy go out with their big dogs to look for wayfarers lost in the heavy storms. If they find a traveler alive, they give him food and shelter until the storm is over and he is ready to continue his journey. The dead are given a decent burial.

In 1932, Pope Pius XI named St. Bernard of Montjoux the patron saint of Alpinists and other mountaineers.

CLEMENT I, POPE, MARTYR

St. Clement, one of the earliest popes (A.D. 100) is credited with having discovered the cloth now known as felt. Before he was pope, Clement was forced to flee from certain persecutors, and as he trudged along the hot dusty road his feet began to blister. To ease his discomfort, he put some wool inside his sandals. When he stopped he discovered that by the motion and pressure of walking he had pounded the wool into a compact sheet. Later he took the time to develop the crude substance into a workable cloth. Because of this legend, Clement became the patron saint of hatters.

Clement is generally thought to be St. Peter's third successor. Little is known of his life, although it is believed that he knew some of the apostles and that he may be the Clement mentioned by St. Paul in his epistle to the Philippians (4:3). Clement may have been a Jew, a freed slave, or the son of a freed slave. It is known that he was well-educated from one of his writings, Letter to the Corinthians, which has been authenticated. On the strength of this letter, Clement is accounted the first of the Apostolic Fathers.

Clement is venerated as a martyr, but there is no proof of his martyrdom. The tale that he was sentenced to hard labor in the Crimea, there lashed to an anchor, and thrown into the sea is legendary, but it became popular and accounts for his many marine dedications. An anchor is his symbol in art.

PRAYER FOR ALL MANKIND

Clement's Letter to the Corinthians ends with a beautiful prayer for all mankind:

God of all flesh, who givest life and death, Thou who castest down the insolence of the proud and turnest aside the scheming of men, be our help!

O Master, appease the hunger of the indigent; deliver the fallen among us.

God, good and merciful, forget our sins, our wrongdoing and backsliding; take no account of the faults of Thy servants.

Give us concord and peace, as to all the inhabitants of the earth.

It is from Thee that our princes and those who govern us here below hold their power; grant them health, peace, concord, stability; direct their counsels in the way of goodness.

Thou alone canst do all this and confer on us still greater benefits.

We proclaim it by the High Priest and Master of our soul,

Jesus Christ, by whom to Thee be all glory and power, now and in endless ages.

DISMAS, CRIMINAL

In St. Luke 23:39-43, we find the brief but eloquent story of the two "malefactors" or thieves who were crucified with Jesus. One of them joined with the crowd to revile the Lord; the other, repentant, He promised "Today shalt thou be with me in Paradise." Popularly, this good thief has been called Dismas. He is the patron of persons condemned to death and of prisoners in general. His day is March 25, but in the United States, the National Catholic Prison Chaplains Association has received special permission from Rome to observe the second Sunday in October as "Good Thief Sunday" and to celebrate Masses in American prisons in honor of St. Dismas.

DUNSTAN, MONK, ARCHBISHOP

A tenth-century Englishman, St. Dunstan was so good that he kept the devil worried, the story goes. Satan felt that the saint's activities had to be watched all the time. Once when Dunstan was working at the monastery forge, he looked up and saw the devil peering at him through the window. Quick as a flash he pulled his red-hot tongs from the coals and grabbed the devil's nose with them. Howling and writhing, the devil ran and dipped his nose in nearby Tunbridge Wells to cool it off. To this day, the water in Tunbridge Wells, according to the English, is sulfur water.

Little is known of Dunstan's early years; he was related to the royal family of Wessex, received a good education at Glastonbury, and became a monk and priest. King Edmund I commissioned him to restore monastic life at Glastonbury, and from this began his revival of organized monasticism in

St. Bartholomew holds tatters of his own skin and the knife used to flay him in his statue in the Basilica of St. John Lateran in Rome.

St. Bernard of Clairvaux nonchalantly holds a demon underfoot as he preaches in this painting by Sebastiano del Piombo (1485-1547).

England, which had ceased to exist since the Scandinavian invasions. Dunstan founded or refounded many abbeys and helped to draw up a national code of monastic observance in line with the Rule of St. Benedict. He was a principal adviser to all the Wessex kings of his time and in 959 was made Archbishop of Canterbury. The present coronation rite of the English sovereign derives from that compiled and used by Dunstan for the coronation of Edgar as king of all England at Bath in 973. In addition to his exhaustive work, he was also credited with being an expert metalworker, a skillful scribe, and a musician. As an old man, he delighted in teaching the boys of the cathedral school at Canterbury, and the students returned his affection as he was a gentle master.

St. Dunstan is the patron of blacksmiths.

FIACRE (OR FIACHRA), HERMIT

In spite of the abundance of statues of St. Francis seen in American gardens, the patron of gardeners is St. Fiacre, a seventh-century hermit priest and a hotheaded Irishman.

One time when he went to see a French bishop, his reputation for impatience preceded him, so the bishop kept him sitting on a rock in the garden all day to teach him a lesson. Apparently he spent the time in devotions; at any rate, after Fiacre's death, the rock was soon discovered to have miraculous powers. The king, sitting where Fiacre had waited for the bishop, was cured of an illness. The news spread quickly and the place became a shrine. Because of the number of pilgrims passing through Paris on their way to the shrine of St. Fiacre, an enterprising Parisian put up a tavern, calling it the Hotel de St. Fiacre. Soon there was a thriving cab business going between the hotel and the shrine. The cabs became known as fiacres, and St. Fiacre by extension became patron of cabdrivers.

Little is known of the origins of this saint. His original Irish name may have been Fiachra. Coming into France, he was kindly received at Meaux by St. Faro, who gave him a piece of land on which to build a hermitage. Fiacre built a cell for himself and a large hospice for travelers. He spent his time in prayer, working with his hands, and caring for the travelers and the poor of the area.

Because of an incident with a meddlesome woman who spoke against him to St. Faro, Fiacre excluded all women from his enclosure. There are many stories of misfortune which befell those who trespassed, even after his death.

Fiacre's fame for miracles was widespread. All manner of diseases were cured by his touch — blindness, fevers, and especially tumors. After his death for many centuries, his chapel and his shrine drew the sick, and his intercession was especially asked for by persons suffering from hemorrhoids.

Fiacre is looked on as the patron saint of gardeners because of the fine vegetables he grew around his hermitage. His emblem in art is a spade.

HOLY INNOCENTS

The Holy Innocents are the male children aged two years and younger who were slaughtered in or near Bethlehem by King Herod's order in hopes that the Messiah would be among them. They are honored as the first to die for Christ, and have been venerated as martyrs from early times.

There have been some highly exaggerated estimates of the number of the children who were killed. It is unlikely that there were more than twenty of them at most.

In Bethlehem, Christian children gathered in the Church of the Nativity in the afternoon to sing a hymn in memory of the Holy Innocents. In the tenth century, the English Aelfric wrote of them as "flowers of martyrdom, the young warriors who bore witness to the Savior whom as yet they did not know."

December 28, Holy Innocents' Day or Childermas, has

traditionally been considered the unluckiest day of the year. Ancient wisdom warns not to promise anything on this day, not to scrub the kitchen, not to trim your fingernails, and above all not to marry. Edward IV of England, on finding that the Sunday set for his coronation was Holy Innocents' Day, moved the ceremony to Monday in order not to start his official reign on that unhappy day.

The Holy Innocents are counted as patrons for choirboys, school children, and orphans.

JOHN BOSCO, FUN-LOVING FOUNDER

"Enjoy yourself as much as you like, if only you keep from sin!" Good advice, and from a saint at that!

What John Bosco realized, and what some people sadly never learn, is that many will be attracted to Christ if those who represent Him have an attractive disposition. Rigid, rude, grumpy people who also claim to be religious are a scandal to the Church. The joy of Christ as shown in the life of this nineteenth-century wonder-worker is a hallmark of the truly religious.

As a youth, John Bosco practiced his skills as a juggler, tightrope walker, ventriloquist, and acrobat in order to attract the attention of his peers. After gaining their admiration and respect, he encouraged them to pray with him. As an adult, the saint's reflection of God's joy was passed on to one of the greatest of the armies of religious in the Church — the Salesian order.

Sympathetically attracted to abandoned and neglected boys, this humble Italian priest established a teaching apostolate that would transform the boys into good, industrious citizens. His work has spread throughout the world.

From the age of nine, the saint was favored with a series of visionary dreams which guided his actions. Pope Pius XI once remarked, "In John Bosco's life the supernatural became the natural and the extraordinary ordinary." In addition to his dreams, the saint was favored with many mystical phenomena such as the gift of prophecy and the ability to multiply food. Having to make night calls at a time of anticlericalism and in dangerous parts of the city of Turin, the saint was often accompanied by a large gray dog which disappeared when the priest returned safely to the rectory. In spite of all the miraculous and mystical facets of his life, by the testimony of all who knew him, the saint maintained a joyful, warm and loving humanity that attracted those around him and allowed him to accomplish his mission of leading them to God.

In spite of his prodigious work of founding institutions for his boys, building churches, and raising funds for these endeavors, he found time to author over a hundred books and pamphlets. In recognition of this accomplishment, he was declared the patron saint of Catholic publishers and editors.

JULIAN, LEGENDARY PENITENT

Julian is called Julian the Hospitaler, or "the Poor Man." Of the many churches, hospitals, and other charitable establishments in Western Europe which bore his name, the large majority commemorate the hero of a romance for whose historical existence there is no solid evidence.

According to the version in the Golden Legend, Julian was a nobleman who through a mistake of identity killed his own father and mother. To expiate for his unwitting crime, he went with his good wife Basilissa to live by a ford across a river where they gave help to travelers and built a refuge for the sick and the poor. One day they took in a man almost dead with cold and tended lovingly to him. Shortly before he disappeared in glory, he told Julian that Jesus had accepted his penance.

Julian is called the patron saint of hospitality. Over the centuries the word hospitality evolved into meaning something different from providing refuge for the sick and the poor, and by the Middle Ages the saint was sometimes portrayed as a party-giving playboy. His hospitality, however, was a deep Christian concern for those in need of help.

There are many saints named Julian, especially among the early martyrs. In some cases, their stories have gotten mixed up with the tale of the Hospitaler and vice versa. St. Julian has been honored as the patron of ferrymen, innkeepers, circus people, and others.

LAWRENCE, DEACON AND MARTYR

"Lazy as Lawrence" used to be a popular expression in England. The somewhat gruesome origin of the saying referred to the execution of St. Lawrence — who, while being roasted over a fire, said to his torturers, "Turn me over now, this side is done."

This saint, for whom the great North American river is named, is surrounded by legend although the facts of his life are sparse. He was born in Aragon (Spain), served Pope Sixtus II as a deacon, and was martyred in the third century.

At the beginning of August 256, the emperor Valerian issued an order that all bishops, deacons, and priests were to be executed. Pope Sixtus II was found and killed, and his persecutors came to claim the Church's possessions. Deacon Lawrence was arrested but asked for three days to gather and inventory the treasures at his command. The time was granted, and he used it to turn all the goods into cash and distribute the money to the needy. On the fourth day, Lawrence came back, followed by a crowd of widows, orphans, lepers, beggars, cripples, children, and old people. He pointed to the crowd and told the judge, "Behold the treasures of the Church!" The judge sentenced him to death by burning in hopes that Lawrence would reveal where he had hidden the Church treasure.

In art, Lawrence is represented holding a gridiron, the instrument on which he met his death. It is preserved in the

Church of San Lorenzo in Rome. The grill is embedded in the wall of the reliquary chapel of the church, which dates from the fifth century and contains the relics of many other early martyrs.

St. Lawrence is one of the most honored martyrs of the early Church. A number of early popes venerated his relics and added to his shrine. Six churches in Rome were built to honor his memory. He is named in the Canon of the Mass. His feast is observed on August 10.

Lawrence is sometimes called the courteous Spaniard. This is from the story that when, two hundred years after his death, his tomb was opened to receive the bones of St. Stephen, the skeleton of St. Lawrence politely moved to the left, giving the place of honor to the distinguished newcomer.

Lawrence is especially invoked by those suffering from lumbago and rheumatism. He is known as patron to cooks, chefs, and restaurant owners.

PAUL MIKI AND COMPANIONS (JAPANESE MARTYRS)

St. Francis Xavier first took Christianity to Japan in 1549, and for a generation the new faith flourished there. In 1588, under the angry leadership of the Emperor Tagosama, an era of persecution began, with thousands of Christians tortured and killed. They were burned, beheaded, crucified, and suspended head-downward over pits of burning sulphur. St. Paul Miki and twenty-five companions were crucified at Nagasaki in 1597.

This representative group of the Japanese martyrs is remembered in the Roman calendar on February 6. Of the group, six were European Franciscan missionaries led by Spanish St. Peter Baptist. St. Paul Miki was a Japanese Jesuit priest, and St. Leo Karasuma was a Korean layman. The remainder were Japanese laymen, of whom three were young boys. They were crucified simultaneously by being raised on crosses and then stabbed with spears.

The persecutions continued for many years, and finally it appeared that there were no Christians left in Japan. What happened, however, is that they had gone underground. Three hundred years later, when Christianity was again permitted in Japan, a priest saying Mass was startled when a stranger came and knelt by him whispering, "My heart is with your heart." Surprised, the priest questioned the stranger and learned that for three centuries this lovely statement had been the secret password by which Christians recognized one another and kept the faith alive.

PEREGRINE, PROTECTOR FROM CANCER

St. Peregrine is not well known in America, and yet he is the patron for sufferers with one of the most dread diseases in our country today — cancer.

Peregrine Laziosi was born into a wealthy family in Forli, Italy, in 1260. As a young man, he was active in anti-papal activities until a chance meeting with St. Philip Benizi caused him to change the direction of his life. He decided to become a priest and joined St. Philip's community, the Servites. St. Peregrine became famous for his preaching and personal holiness, sought out as a confessor. He contracted cancer of the foot, which besides being painful gave off a gangrenous stench so foul that it was repulsive to his associates. At last the cancer advanced to such a point that doctors wanted to amputate his foot to save his life.

The night before the operation was spent in trustful prayer to God. Peregrine crawled into the monastery chapel and offered a prayer of resignation along with the plea that his leg would not be amputated. He fell asleep before the image of the crucified Savior, and in a dream Christ seemed to stretch out His hand from the crucifix and touch his diseased leg. On awakening, Peregrine discovered that his cancer was completely cured.

This miracle greatly enhanced the reputation this holy man had already acquired by his exemplary life, and it gave faith to those fearing cancer or suffering from it or any form of running sores. His personal sanctity bore fruit in many miracles; he healed the sick and converted hardened sinners. Peregrine is invoked and well known in Austria, Bavaria, Hungary, Italy, and Spain. Spanish Catholics speak of him as a wonder-worker.

Peregrine was canonized in 1726 by Pope Benedict XIII. His body was exhumed and found incorrupt. In contrast to the once foul stench of his cancer, the body emitted a heavenly odor which was described as an overwhelming fragrance of flowers. The body is still preserved intact.

URSULA AND THE VIRGINS

The legend of Ursula tells of a beautiful princess of Cornwall whose fame reached a Scottish prince named Conan. He sent for her to come and marry him, requesting her to bring other girls to marry the Christian soldiers with him. She immediately set sail with ten or eleven thousand eligible young ladies, but their boats were driven off course up the Rhine river, where they were all killed by barbarian Huns against whom they defended their virtue at Cologne in 383.

It is far more likely that Ursula was accompanied by ten or eleven companions. The large number mentioned in her legend probably stems from the twelfth-century discovery of a vast quantity of human bones at Cologne. What was found was probably an old Roman cemetery, but popular opinion made the bones the remains of the ill-fated bridal party.

An interesting sequel to this story is found in our own state of Louisiana. In the seventeenth century, Louisiana belonged to France, and the king sent boatloads of girls to marry the lonely settlers. Each girl was given the "King's dowry," a small chest containing one blanket, four sheets, two pair of stockings, six headdresses, and a "pelisse" or fur-trimmed coat. The arrival of

Statue of St. John Bosco with children at the Salesian shrine in New Rochelle, N.Y. Don Bosco died in 1888 and was canonized in 1934.

In this typical Italian holy card, St. Lawrence, patron of cooks and chefs, is shown with the gridiron on which he was said to be roasted.

these "casket girls" in New Orleans was celebrated with a procession in honor of St. Ursula, and they were housed in the Ursuline convent while waiting for the young men to make their choices.

VITUS, MARTYR, AND THE DANCE

Very little is known about this early martyr who is said to have been put to death in 303 for the faith, along with his tutor Modestus and his governess Crescentia. There are various explanations of how his name came to be associated with the disease of chorea or "St. Vitus's Dance." One story is that there was a shrine to him in Germany and people believed that anyone who danced in front of this shrine on his feast day would be assured of good health for the coming year. Some dancers danced with such tremendous enthusiasm that their jerky, hysterical movements resembled those of patients suffering from chorea. He is the patron of all who have chorea, epilepsy, and all diseases connected with nervous shaking and muscular spasms, and he is also invoked against rabies and sleeping sickness.

In the eighth century, St. Vitus's relics were brought to France and later to the Abbey of Corvey in the East Frankish Kingdom. This abbey was a center of great missionary activity, and the monks there introduced the veneration of St. Vitus to the Germanic and Slavic tribes. His cultus soon spread all over France, Germany, England, Scandinavia, and Eastern Europe. By the thirteenth century he was venerated in all these countries, and many churches were built in his honor. His feast was celebrated with pilgrimages, rest from work, and merry festivals.

In the strange "epidemics" of dancing mania that swept Western Europe at various times from the fourteenth to the sixteenth centuries, St. Vitus's patronage grew to gigantic proportions. The victims of that mass hysteria were brought to his shrines and led three times around his altar or statue to obtain relief or cure.*

Originally St. Vitus's patronage was restricted to the morbid forms of dancing. Eventually it was extended to cover real performances and he became known as a patron of dancers and actors.

In art, St. Vitus is often pictured with a chicken. In medieval times, it was a custom to bring roosters, hens and eggs as gifts to his shrines. He is also often pictured with a dog.

Note
* Weiser, *The Holyday Book* (New York, 1956), p. 170.

Bibliography

Alberione, Rev. James. *Mary, Mother and Model*. Boston: St. Paul Editions, 1962.

Attwater, Donald. *The Avenel Dictionary of Saints*. New York: Avenel Books, 1981.

Ball, Ann. *Handbook of Catholic Sacramentals*. Huntington, Indiana: Our Sunday Visitor, Inc., 1991.

_____. *Modern Saints: Their Lives and Faces* (3 vols.). Rockford, Illinois: TAN Books, 1983.

Carroll, Anne W. *Christ the King: Lord of History*. Manassas, Virginia: Trinity Communications, 1986.

Christopher, Rev. Joseph P., and Spence, Very Rev. Charles E., ed. *The Raccolta*. New York: Benziger Brothers, 1943.

Cruz, Joan Carroll. *Relics*. Huntington, Indiana: Our Sunday Visitor, Inc., 1984.

_____. *Secular Saints*. Rockford, Illinois: TAN Books, 1989.

Delaney, John J. *Dictionary of Saints*. New York: Doubleday and Company, 1980.

Fantony, Natalie. "Valentines." *New Book of Knowledge*. New York, Canada: Grolier, 1968, p. 266.

Farmer, David Hugh. *The Oxford Dictionary of Saints*. New York: Oxford University Press, 1987.

Frazer, Sir James George. *The Golden Bough*. New York: Macmillan Publishing Company, 1932, 1940, 1963.

Freze, Michael, S.F.O. *The Making of Saints*. Huntington, Indiana: Our Sunday Visitor, Inc., 1991.

Gaster, Theodore H., ed. *The New Golden Bough*. New York: S.G. Phillips, 1972.

Gregory, Lady Augusta. *A Book of Saints and Wonders Put Down Here by Lady Gregory According to the Old Writings and the Memory of the People of Ireland*. New York: Oxford University Press, 1971.

Hanley, Boniface, O.F.M. "All He Could Do Was Pray." *The Anthonian.* Paterson, New Jersey: St. Anthony's Guild, Vol. 53, No. 3, 1979.

_____. *That Martin Girl.* Paterson, New Jersey: St. Anthony's Guild, 1979.

Harper, Howard V. *Days and Customs of All Faiths.* New York: Fleet Publishing Corporation, 1957.

Hoagland, Victor. C.P. *The Book of Saints.* New York: Regina Press, 1986.

Hoever, Rev. Hugo, O.C.S.O. *Lives of the Saints.* New York: Catholic Book Publishing Co., 1977.

_____. *Saint Joseph Daily Missal.* New York: Catholic Book Publishing Co., 1963.

Kalberer, Augustine, O.S.B. *Lives of the Saints.* Chicago: Franciscan Herald Press, 1976.

Kleinz, Msgr. John P. *The Who's Who of Heaven.* Westminster, Maryland: Christian Classics, 1987.

Knowles, Leo. *Saints Who Changed Things.* St. Paul: Carillon Books, 1977.

Liptak, Rev. David Q. *More Saints for Our Time.* Waldwick, New Jersey: Arena Lettres, 1983.

NA. *The Little Treasury of St. Anthony.* Paterson, New Jersey: St. Anthony's Guild, 1962.

Lovasik, Rev. Lawrence G., S.V.D. *Saint Anthony of Padua.* New York: Catholic Book Publishing Co., 1984.

NA. *Manual of Piety for the Use of the Brothers of the Christian Schools.* New York: La Salle Bureau, 1951.

Maschio, Rev. Aurelius, S.D.B. *St. Anthony of Padua.* Bombay: Don Bosco, 1981.

Moran, Patrick R., ed. *Day by Day with the Saints.* Huntington, Indiana: Our Sunday Visitor, Inc., 1985.

Riva, Anna. *Devotions to the Saints.* Toluca Lake, California: International Imports, 1982.

NA. *St. Joseph Today.* St. Louis, Missouri: Work of St. Joseph, 1974.

Seculoff, Rev. James. *Catholic Home Devotions.* Huntington,
   Indiana: Our Sunday Visitor, Inc., 1986.

Shereley-Price, Leo, trans. *Bede's History of the English
   Church and People.* New York: Penguin Books, 1978.

Smith, Gary. "St. Joseph, Realtor?" *Catholic Digest.* St. Paul:
   University of St. Thomas, March 1991.

Stravinskas, Rev. Peter, ed. *Our Sunday Visitor's Catholic
   Encyclopedia.* Huntington, Indiana: Our Sunday Visitor,
   Inc., 1991.

Voragine, Jacobus de. *The Golden Legend.* New York:
   Longmans, Green and Co., 1969.

Webling, Peggy. *Saints and Their Stories.* New York:
   Frederick A. Stokes Company, 1920.

Weiser, Francis X. *Handbook of Christian Feasts and Customs.*
   New York: Harcourt, Brace and World, Inc. 1958.

_____. *The Holyday Book.* New York: Harcourt, Brace
   and Company, 1956.

Wilson, Stephen, ed. *Saints and Their Cults.* Cambridge,
   England: Cambridge University Press, 1983.

Woodward, Kenneth L. *Making Saints.* New York: Simon and
   Schuster, 1990.

Correspondence and Thank You

This book would not have been possible without the help of many people whose assistance, good wishes, and prayers were freely given. In particular I would like to thank the following. If I have missed someone through oversight, I pray that St. Joseph will personally give them my thanks.

Rev. Nelson Aguila, S.A.C., St. Jude Shrine, Baltimore, Md.
Joanna Ball, Houston, Tex.
Sam Ball, Houston, Tex.
Ora Bolton, Jacksonville, Tex.
Rev. John Boscoe, Our Lady of Guadalupe Church, Rosenburg, Tex.
Rev. John Catoir, The Christophers, Inc., New York, N.Y.
Tom Claridge, Religious Books, Victoria, B.C., Canada
Celeste Cottingham, Corpus Christi Library, Houston, Tex.
Rev. Sean Coughlan, O. Carm., Whitefriar St. Church, Dublin, Ireland
Charles Davenport (deceased), Adelphi, Md.
Albert DiBella, Knights of Columbus, Galveston, Tex.
Franciscan Mission Associates, Mt. Vernon, N.Y.
Rev. James Gaunt, C.S.B., St. Basil's Novitiate, Houston, Tex.
Steve Gustafson, Louisville, Ky.
Mary Ellen Hall, Houston Baptist University, Houston, Tex.
Kerry Hawkins, Ellicott City, Md.
Rev. M.M. Herttna, National Shrine of St. Dymphna, Massillon, Ohio
Gracie Lofaro, Galveston, Tex.
Rev. Michael Miller, Vatican City, Europe
Rev. Thaddeus Murphy, O.P., Dominican Friars Guild, New York, N.Y.
National Shrine of St. Jude, Chicago, Ill.
Rev. David Polek, C.Ss.R., Liguori Publications, Liguori, Mo.

Rev. Christopher Rengers, O.F.M. Cap., The Work of St. Joseph, Washington, D.C.

Sister Rita Roethele, Director, Providence Center, Saint-Mary-of-the-Woods, Ind.

St. Jude Children's Research Hospital, Memphis, Tenn.

Salesian Missions, New Rochelle, N.Y.

Rev. Kevin Shanley, O.Carm., Aylsford, Darien, Ill.

Bob Sontrop, London, Ont., Canada

Brother David Tejada, St. Michael's High School, Santa Fe, N.M.